DELICIOUS SLOW COOKER RECIPES FOR ONE

Quick and Healthy Meals Cookbook with Mouthwatering Pictures

by Clara Levine

INTRODUCTION

Are you a solo diner looking for an effortless way to enjoy homemade, nutritious meals? "Delicious Slow Cooker Recipes for One: Quick and Healthy Meals Cookbook with Mouthwatering Pictures" by Clara Levine is here to revolutionize your mealtime.

Navigating meal prep and cooking for one can be challenging, often leading to repetitive meals or reliance on fast food. Clara Levine's collection of slow cooker recipes is meticulously designed for individuals who love good food but have little time or desire to cook complex dishes every day. This cookbook offers a variety of recipes that cater to all tastes and dietary needs, ensuring that cooking for one is never dull but always healthy, quick, and delicious.

Imagine the joy of coming home to a warm, ready-to-eat meal that requires minimal prep and virtually no cleanup. From tender meats and hearty stews to vegetarian delights and sweet treats, these recipes are perfect for any day of the week. Accompanied by mouthwatering pictures, each dish is a feast for the taste buds and the eyes, inspiring you to try new flavors and ingredients. This cookbook promises to make your solo dining experience both satisfying and exciting.

Take the first step towards transforming your solo meals into a delightful and effortless experience. Whether you're a busy professional, a student, or simply someone who enjoys the simplicity and comfort of slow-cooked meals, "Delicious Slow Cooker Recipes for One" is your companion in the kitchen. Available in both Kindle and Paperback formats, grab your copy today and start enjoying the art of cooking for one with Clara Levine's expert guidance and exquisite recipes. Happy cooking!

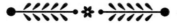

TABLE OF CONTENTS

CHAPTER 01: SEA DELIGHTS

Recipe 01: Shrimp Scampi

Dive into the sumptuous flavors of "Shrimp Scampi with Garlic and Butter Sauce," a luxurious dish from our Slow Cooker Cookbook. This recipe features succulent shrimp bathed in a rich garlic and butter sauce, finished with a sprinkle of fresh parsley for a touch of brightness. Ideal for a decadent solo meal, it promises an elegant dining experience that's surprisingly easy to prepare, making it perfect for a special night.

Servings: 1

Prepping Time: 10 minutes

Cook Time: 2 hours

Difficulty: Easy

Ingredients:

- ✓ 1/2 lb shrimp, peeled and deveined
- ✓ 3 tablespoons butter
- ✓ 2 cloves garlic, minced
- ✓ Salt and pepper to taste
- ✓ 1 tablespoon lemon juice
- ✓ Fresh parsley, chopped, for garnish

Step-by-Step Preparation:

1. Place shrimp in the slow cooker.
2. In a small saucepan, melt butter over medium heat. Add garlic and sauté until fragrant.
3. Pour the garlic butter over the shrimp. Season with salt and pepper.
4. Cook on low for 2 hours until shrimp are pink and tender.
5. Stir in lemon juice just before serving.
6. Garnish with fresh parsley.

Nutritional Facts: (Per serving)

- ❖ Calories: 330
- ❖ Protein: 24g
- ❖ Carbohydrates: 2g
- ❖ Fat: 25g
- ❖ Sodium: 880mg
- ❖ Fiber: 0g

Conclude your dining experience with Shrimp Scampi with Garlic and Butter Sauce. This dish captures the essence of fine dining with the comfort of home cooking. Whether enjoyed as a lavish treat for yourself or impressing a guest, this recipe from our Slow Cooker Cookbook offers a delightful way to savor the luxurious combination of shrimp, garlic, and butter, all from the comfort of your kitchen.

Recipe 02: Sea Bass Fillet

Indulge in the exquisite blend of flavors with "Sea Bass Fillet with Tomato, Hot Chili Pepper, and Asparagus," a gourmet dish from our Slow Cooker Cookbook. This recipe showcases the delicate sea bass in a lively sauce of tomato and fiery chili pepper, accompanied by tender asparagus. Ideal for those seeking a sophisticated yet easy-to-prepare meal, it's a culinary delight that promises a burst of flavors in a harmonious balance, perfect for a special dinner for one.

Servings: 1

Cook Time: 2 hours

Prepping Time: 10 minutes

Difficulty: Easy

Ingredients:

- ✓ 1 sea bass fillet
- ✓ 1 tomato, diced
- ✓ 1 hot chili pepper, finely sliced
- ✓ 5 asparagus spears, trimmed
- ✓ 1 tablespoon olive oil
- ✓ Salt and pepper to taste
- ✓ Lemon wedges for serving

Step-by-Step Preparation:

1. Place the sea bass fillet in the slow cooker.
2. Surround with diced tomato and asparagus spears.
3. Scatter sliced hot chili pepper over the top.
4. Drizzle everything with olive oil and season with salt and pepper.
5. Cook on low for 2 hours, until the fish is tender and the vegetables are cooked.
6. Serve hot, accompanied by lemon wedges.

Nutritional Facts: (Per serving)

- ❖ Calories: 320
- ❖ Protein: 28g
- ❖ Carbohydrates: 12g
- ❖ Fat: 18g
- ❖ Sodium: 80mg
- ❖ Fiber: 4g

Conclude your dining experience with Sea Bass Fillet with Tomato, Hot Chili Pepper, and Asparagus. This dish elegantly combines the freshness of the sea with the vibrancy of vegetables and spices. Whether you're treating yourself to a luxurious meal or impressing a guest, this recipe from our Slow Cooker Cookbook delivers a sophisticated, flavorful, and healthful option that will captivate and satisfy you.

Recipe 03: Tilapia Fish Veracruz

Immerse yourself in the vibrant flavors of "Tilapia Fish Prepared Veracruz Style," a gem from our Slow Cooker Cookbook. This dish marries the delicate taste of tilapia with the boldness of tomatoes, the earthiness of potatoes, and the salty accents of capers and olives, creating a symphony of flavors reminiscent of Mexican coastal cuisine. Perfect for anyone seeking a meal that's both simple and bursting with flavor, it's an exquisite choice for a solo gourmet adventure.

Servings: 1

Prepping Time: 15 minutes

Cook Time: 4 hours

Difficulty: Easy

Ingredients:

- ✓ 1 tilapia fillet
- ✓ 1 potato, thinly sliced
- ✓ 1 tomato, sliced
- ✓ 1 tablespoon capers
- ✓ 1/4 cup olives, sliced
- ✓ 1/2 onion, sliced
- ✓ 1 clove garlic, minced
- ✓ Salt and pepper to taste
- ✓ 1/4 cup water
- ✓ Fresh cilantro for garnish

Step-by-Step Preparation:

1. Layer the bottom of the slow cooker with sliced potatoes.
2. Place the tilapia fillet on top of the potatoes.
3. Arrange tomato slices, capers, olives, onion, and garlic around and on top of the fish.
4. Season with salt and pepper, then add water to the cooker.
5. Cook on low for 4 hours, until the fish is tender and the vegetables are cooked.
6. Garnish with fresh cilantro before serving.

Nutritional Facts: (Per serving)

- ❖ Calories: 350
- ❖ Protein: 25g
- ❖ Carbohydrates: 40g
- ❖ Fat: 10g
- ❖ Sodium: 300mg
- ❖ Fiber: 5g

Conclude your dining experience with Tilapia Fish Prepared Veracruz Style. This dish brings the essence of Veracruz to your table. Whether you're a fan of Mexican cuisine or exploring new flavors, this recipe from our Slow Cooker Cookbook offers a deliciously unique way to enjoy tilapia, promising a meal that's as nutritious as it is flavorful.

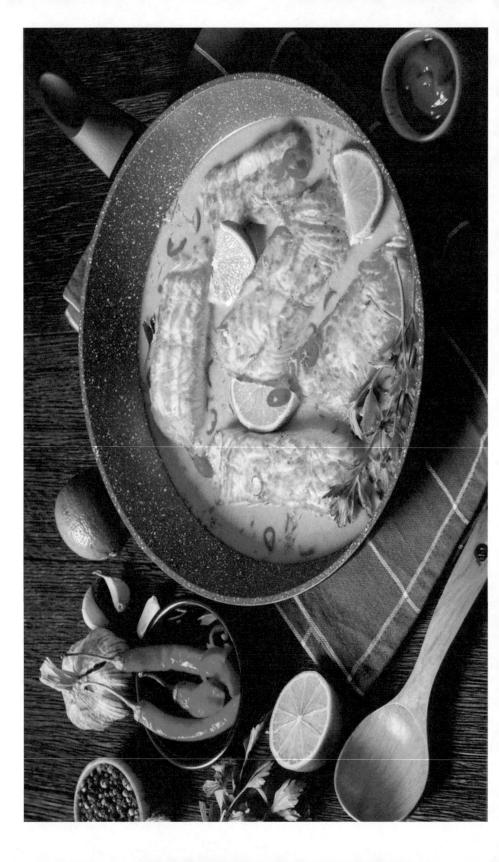

Recipe 04: Salmon in Coconut Lime Sauce

Embark on a culinary voyage with "Salmon Fish Curry in Coconut Lime Sauce," a standout dish from our Slow Cooker Cookbook. This recipe beautifully combines the rich flavors of salmon with a creamy coconut lime sauce, spiced to perfection, offering a lush and aromatic experience. Ideal for those craving a meal that balances hearty substance with exotic flair, it's a perfect solo indulgence that brings the tropics' tastes to your plate.

Servings: 1

Cook Time: 3 hours

Prepping Time: 15 minutes

Difficulty: Easy

Ingredients:

- ✓ 1 salmon fillet
- ✓ 1 cup coconut milk
- ✓ Juice and zest of 1 lime
- ✓ 1 teaspoon curry powder
- ✓ 1/2 teaspoon turmeric
- ✓ 1/2 teaspoon ginger, minced
- ✓ Salt to taste
- ✓ Fresh cilantro for garnish
- ✓ 1 chili pepper, sliced (optional)

Step-by-Step Preparation:

1. Place the salmon fillet in the slow cooker.
2. Mix coconut milk, lime juice and zest, curry powder, turmeric, ginger, and salt in a bowl.
3. Pour the mixture over the salmon.
4. Cook on low for 3 hours, until the salmon is cooked through and flaky.
5. Garnish with fresh cilantro and sliced chili pepper for an extra kick.

Nutritional Facts: (Per serving)

- ❖ Calories: 400
- ❖ Protein: 25g
- ❖ Carbohydrates: 6g
- ❖ Fat: 32g
- ❖ Sodium: 200mg
- ❖ Fiber: 1g

Conclude your meal with Salmon Fish Curry in Coconut Lime Sauce. This dish promises a delightful exploration of flavors and textures. Whether you're seeking to impress your palate or indulge in a luxurious meal, this recipe from our Slow Cooker Cookbook offers a delectable way to enjoy salmon, ensuring a memorable and satisfying dining experience.

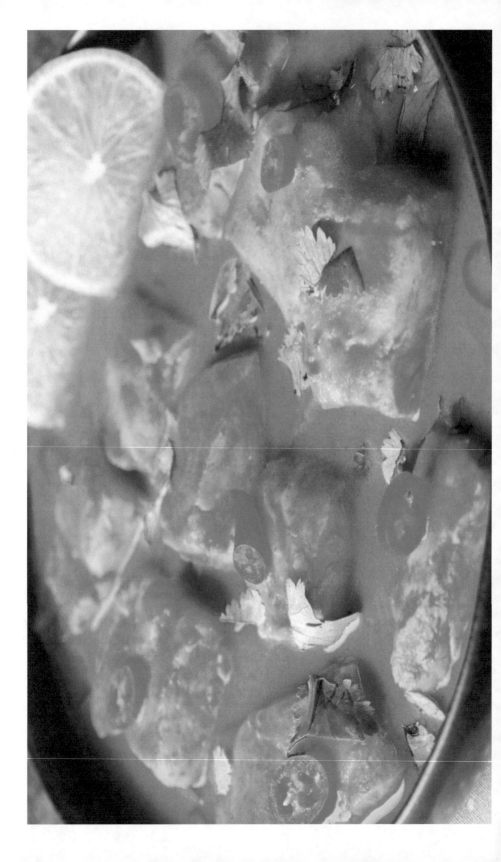

Recipe 05: Fragrant Fish Curry

Explore the aromatic depths of "Fragrant Fish Curry of White Fish Fillet with Coconut, Tomatoes, and Asian Spices," a culinary masterpiece from our Slow Cooker Cookbook. This dish encapsulates the essence of Asian cuisine, blending succulent white fish with the richness of coconut, the tanginess of tomatoes, and a medley of exotic spices. Perfect for those who appreciate a symphony of flavors, it's a soulful meal that promises a journey for your senses, crafted with care for a solo dining experience.

Servings: 1

Cook Time: 4 hours

Prepping Time: 15 minutes

Difficulty: Medium

Ingredients:

- ✓ 1 white fish fillet (such as cod or tilapia)
- ✓ 1 cup coconut milk
- ✓ 1 tomato, chopped
- ✓ 1 onion, finely sliced
- ✓ 2 cloves garlic, minced
- ✓ 1 teaspoon turmeric
- ✓ 1 teaspoon cumin
- ✓ 1 teaspoon coriander
- ✓ 1/2 teaspoon chili powder
- ✓ Salt to taste
- ✓ Fresh cilantro for garnish
- ✓ Lime wedges for serving

Step-by-Step Preparation:

1. Place the fish fillet in the slow cooker.
2. Scatter the chopped tomato, sliced onion, and minced garlic around and on top of the fish.
3. Mix coconut milk with turmeric, cumin, coriander, chili powder, and salt in a bowl. Pour this mixture over the fish.
4. Cook on low for 4 hours until the fish is tender and the flavors have melded.
5. Garnish with fresh cilantro and serve with lime wedges on the side.

Nutritional Facts: (Per serving)

- ❖ Calories: 320
- ❖ Protein: 22g
- ❖ Carbohydrates: 12g
- ❖ Fat: 22g
- ❖ Sodium: 200mg
- ❖ Fiber: 3g

Conclude your dining experience with a Fragrant Fish Curry of White Fish Fillet. This dish nourishes and mesmerizes with its complexity and depth. Whether you're a connoisseur of Asian cuisine or seeking a new culinary adventure, this recipe from our Slow Cooker Cookbook delivers an exquisite blend of flavors and textures, making it an exceptional meal for any occasion.

Recipe 06: Fish in Dried Red Curry

Embark on a culinary journey with "Fish in Dried Red Curry," a bold and vibrant dish from our Slow Cooker Cookbook. This recipe offers a unique twist on traditional curry, featuring a piece of tender fish infused with the intense flavors of dried red curry paste and a blend of aromatic spices. Perfect for those seeking a meal that's both exotic and easy to prepare, it's a solo dining delight that brings the rich taste of Southeast Asia to your kitchen.

Servings: 1

Prepping Time: 10 minutes

Cook Time: 3 hours

Difficulty: Medium

Ingredients:

- ✓ 1 fish fillet (such as cod or snapper)
- ✓ 2 tablespoons dried red curry paste
- ✓ 1 cup coconut milk
- ✓ 1/2 bell pepper, sliced
- ✓ 1/4 onion, sliced
- ✓ 1 tablespoon fish sauce
- ✓ 1 teaspoon sugar
- ✓ Salt to taste
- ✓ Basil leaves, for garnish
- ✓ Lime wedges for serving

Step-by-Step Preparation:

1. Place the fish fillet in the slow cooker.
2. Mix the red curry paste with coconut milk, fish sauce, and sugar in a bowl until well combined.
3. Pour the curry mixture over the fish. Add sliced bell pepper and onion.
4. Cook on low for 3 hours, until the fish is cooked and the sauce is flavorful.
5. Season with salt to taste.
6. Garnish with basil leaves and serve with lime wedges on the side.

Nutritional Facts: (Per serving)

- ❖ Calories: 400
- ❖ Protein: 25g
- ❖ Carbohydrates: 15g
- ❖ Fat: 28g
- ❖ Sodium: 700mg
- ❖ Fiber: 2g

Conclude your meal with Fish in Dried Red Curry, a dish that promises an unforgettable flavor adventure. Whether you're a lover of spicy food or eager to explore the nuances of curry, this recipe from our Slow Cooker Cookbook offers a delightful way to enjoy the complexity of dried red curry, ensuring a flavorful and satisfying culinary experience.

Recipe 07: Salmon Steak

Indulge in the savory delight of "Salmon Steak with Gravy and Lemon," a refined dish from our Slow Cooker Cookbook. This recipe showcases a succulent salmon steak drizzled with a rich, flavorful gravy and brightened by a squeeze of fresh lemon. It's perfect for anyone seeking a gourmet meal that's both straightforward to prepare and impressively delicious, offering a balance of flavors to please the palate.

Servings: 1   **Cook Time:** 2 hours

Prepping Time: 10 minutes   **Difficulty:** Easy

Ingredients:

- ✓ 1 salmon steak
- ✓ 1/2 cup chicken or fish broth
- ✓ 2 tablespoons lemon juice
- ✓ 1 tablespoon butter
- ✓ 1 teaspoon flour
- ✓ Salt and pepper to taste
- ✓ Lemon slices, for garnish

Step-by-Step Preparation:

1. Season the salmon steak with salt and pepper, and place it in the slow cooker.
2. Pour broth and lemon juice over the salmon.
3. Cook on low for 2 hours until salmon is tender and flaky.
4. Near the end of cooking, melt butter in a pan, stir in flour to make a roux, then gradually whisk in cooking juices to make gravy.
5. Serve the salmon steak covered in gravy garnished with lemon slices.

Nutritional Facts: (Per serving)

- ❖ Calories: 320
- ❖ Protein: 23g
- ❖ Carbohydrates: 2g
- ❖ Fat: 24g
- ❖ Sodium: 570mg
- ❖ Fiber: 0g

Conclude your dining experience with Salmon Steak with Gravy and Lemon. This dish combines the simplicity of slow cooking with the elegance of fine dining. Whether you're looking to treat yourself or impress a guest, this recipe from our Slow Cooker Cookbook delivers a deliciously sophisticated meal, ensuring a memorable and flavorful feast.

Recipe 08: Seafood Risotto

Embark on a culinary voyage with "Seafood Risotto with Shrimps, Curry, and Herbs," a sophisticated dish from our Slow Cooker Cookbook. This risotto melds the succulence of shrimp with the exotic warmth of curry and the freshness of aromatic herbs, creating a luxurious and comforting meal. Ideal for those who savor the elegance of Italian cuisine with a twist, it's a single-serving feast that promises a rich tapestry of flavors, ideally suited for an indulgent night in.

Servings: 1

Prepping Time: 15 minutes

Cook Time: 2 hours

Difficulty: Medium

Ingredients:

- ✓ 1/2 cup Arborio rice
- ✓ 1 cup chicken or vegetable broth
- ✓ 1/4 lb shrimps, peeled and deveined
- ✓ 1 teaspoon curry powder
- ✓ 1 tablespoon olive oil
- ✓ 1/4 onion, finely chopped
- ✓ 1 clove garlic, minced
- ✓ Salt and pepper to taste
- ✓ Fresh herbs (parsley, cilantro), chopped, for garnish

Step-by-Step Preparation:

1. Heat olive oil in a pan, sauté onion and garlic until translucent.
2. Add Arborio rice, stirring until grains are coated with oil.
3. Transfer the rice mixture to the slow cooker. Pour in broth and add curry powder.
4. Cook on low for 1.5 hours, stirring occasionally.
5. Add shrimp in the last 30 minutes of cooking.
6. Season with salt and pepper.
7. Serve garnished with fresh herbs.

Nutritional Facts: (Per serving)

- ❖ Calories: 450
- ❖ Protein: 25g
- ❖ Carbohydrates: 65g
- ❖ Fat: 10g
- ❖ Sodium: 900mg
- ❖ Fiber: 2g

Conclude your meal with Seafood Risotto with shrimp, Curry, and Herbs, a dish that nourishes and delights with its complexity and depth. Whether you're a risotto fan or a seafood lover, this recipe from our Slow Cooker Cookbook provides a delectable way to explore the fusion of traditional Italian cooking with the bold flavors of curry.

Recipe 09: Pasta With Tuna and Vegetables

Embark on a flavorful journey with "Pasta with Tuna, Tomato, and Vegetables," a vibrant dish from our Slow Cooker Cookbook. This recipe elevates the humble pasta to a nutritious feast by blending it with flaky tuna, juicy tomatoes, and fresh vegetables. Perfect for the solo diner seeking a satisfying and simple meal, it's a culinary delight that combines healthfulness with heartiness, promising a delicious and balanced experience in every bite.

Servings: 1

Cook Time: 2 hours

Prepping Time: 10 minutes

Difficulty: Easy

Ingredients:

- ✓ 1/2 cup pasta (choice of shape)
- ✓ 1 can tuna in olive oil, drained
- ✓ 1/2 cup diced tomatoes
- ✓ 1/2 cup mixed vegetables (e.g., bell peppers, zucchini)

- ✓ 1 garlic clove, minced
- ✓ 1 tablespoon olive oil
- ✓ Salt and pepper to taste
- ✓ Fresh herbs (basil or parsley) for garnish

Step-by-Step Preparation:

1. Combine pasta, tuna, diced tomatoes, mixed vegetables, and minced garlic in the slow cooker.
2. Drizzle with olive oil and season with salt and pepper.
3. Add enough water or vegetable broth to cover the ingredients.
4. Cook on low for 2 hours or until pasta is tender and flavors have melded.
5. Stir the pasta mixture well. Adjust seasoning if necessary.
6. Garnish with fresh herbs before serving.

Nutritional Facts: (Per serving)

- ❖ Calories: 420
- ❖ Protein: 30g
- ❖ Carbohydrates: 50g

- ❖ Fat: 12g
- ❖ Sodium: 580mg
- ❖ Fiber: 6g

Conclude your meal with pasta with tuna, tomatoes, and vegetables. This dish showcases the ease and elegance of combining straightforward ingredients into a sumptuous dinner. Whether you're a busy professional or simply a lover of good food, this recipe offers a delightful way to enjoy a wholesome, hearty meal without the fuss, ensuring a pleasurable dining experience every time.

Recipe 10: Stewed Calamari Squid Rings

Savor the ocean's depths with "Stewed Squid Rings with Tomato Sauce," a succulent dish from our Slow Cooker Cookbook. This recipe delicately combines tender squid rings with a rich, hearty tomato sauce, creating a comforting and flavorful meal. Perfect for anyone who appreciates seafood's delicate nuances, it offers a simple yet sophisticated dining experience, highlighting the squid's natural sweetness against the robust backdrop of tomato sauce.

Servings: 1

Prepping Time: 15 minutes

Cook Time: 4 hours

Difficulty: Easy

Ingredients:

- ✓ 1/2 lb squid rings
- ✓ 1 cup canned tomato sauce
- ✓ 1/2 onion, finely chopped
- ✓ 1 clove garlic, minced
- ✓ 1 teaspoon dried oregano
- ✓ Salt and pepper to taste
- ✓ Olive oil for sautéing
- ✓ Fresh parsley, chopped, for garnish

Step-by-Step Preparation:

1. Sauté onion and garlic in olive oil until translucent.
2. Add squid rings, stirring gently to combine.
3. Pour tomato sauce over the squid. Season with oregano, salt, and pepper.
4. Transfer to the slow cooker. Cook on low for 4 hours until squid is tender.
5. Serve garnished with fresh parsley.

Nutritional Facts: (Per serving)

- ❖ Calories: 300
- ❖ Protein: 25g
- ❖ Carbohydrates: 15g
- ❖ Fat: 15g
- ❖ Sodium: 700mg
- ❖ Fiber: 3g

Conclude your meal with Stewed Squid Rings with Tomato Sauce. This dish effortlessly marries the simplicity of slow cooking with the exquisite flavors of the sea. Whether you're seeking a comforting seafood meal or a new recipe to add to your culinary repertoire, this dish from our Slow Cooker Cookbook promises a delightful and satisfying experience, making it a perfect choice for any occasion.

CHAPTER 02: MEAT MAGIC

Recipe 01: Beef Stroganoff

Indulge in the rich and comforting flavors of "Beef Stroganoff," a delectable dish from our Slow Cooker Cookbook. This recipe transforms simple ingredients into a luxurious meal, combining tender beef strips in a creamy, tangy sauce perfectly complemented by crisp potatoes. Ideal for those seeking a hearty and satisfying solo meal, it's a gourmet experience that promises to delight your taste buds with its depth of flavor and texture.

Servings: 1

Cook Time: 6 hours

Prepping Time: 15 minutes

Difficulty: Medium

Ingredients:

- ✓ 1/2 lb beef, cut into thin strips
- ✓ 1/4 cup sour cream
- ✓ 2 tablespoons tomato paste
- ✓ 1/2 onion, sliced
- ✓ 1 clove garlic, minced
- ✓ 1/2 cup beef broth
- ✓ Salt and pepper to taste
- ✓ 1 large potato, sliced thinly
- ✓ Olive oil for frying

Step-by-Step Preparation:

1. Season beef strips with salt and pepper and place in the slow cooker.
2. Mix sour cream, tomato paste, onion, garlic, and beef broth; pour over beef.
3. Cook on low for 6 hours until meat is tender.
4. Before serving, fry potato slices in olive oil until crisp.
5. Serve beef topped with its creamy sauce alongside crisp potatoes.

Nutritional Facts: (Per serving)

- ❖ Calories: 550
- ❖ Protein: 40g
- ❖ Carbohydrates: 35g
- ❖ Fat: 30g
- ❖ Sodium: 500mg
- ❖ Fiber: 5g

Conclude your meal with Thin Strips of Beef Cooked in Sour Cream and Tomato Paste, a dish that marries simplicity with elegance. Whether it's a quiet dinner at home or a special occasion, this recipe from our Slow Cooker Cookbook provides a perfect way to enjoy a classic combination of flavors, ensuring a memorable and cozy dining experience.

Recipe 02: Moroccan Lamb Tajine

Embark on a culinary journey to North Africa with "Moroccan Lamb Tagine with Green Olives and Carrots," a vibrant dish from our Slow Cooker Cookbook. This exquisite recipe infuses tender lamb with the aromatic spices of Morocco, complemented by the tangy taste of green olives and the sweetness of carrots. Perfect for a soulful dining experience, it's an ideal choice for those who crave the exotic flavors of distant lands, all while enjoying the comfort of home.

Servings: 1

Prepping Time: 20 minutes

Cook Time: 8 hours

Difficulty: Medium

Ingredients:

- ✓ 1/2 lb lamb, cut into chunks
- ✓ 1/2 cup green olives
- ✓ 2 carrots, sliced
- ✓ 1 onion, chopped
- ✓ 2 cloves garlic, minced
- ✓ 1 teaspoon cumin
- ✓ 1 teaspoon paprika
- ✓ 1/2 teaspoon cinnamon
- ✓ Salt and pepper to taste
- ✓ 1 cup water
- ✓ Fresh cilantro for garnish

Step-by-Step Preparation:

1. Place lamb, carrots, onion, and garlic in the slow cooker.
2. Season with cumin, paprika, cinnamon, salt, and pepper.
3. Add green olives and pour water over the mixture.
4. Cook on low for 8 hours until lamb is tender and flavors meld.
5. Garnish with fresh cilantro before serving.

Nutritional Facts: (Per serving)

- ❖ Calories: 600
- ❖ Protein: 45g
- ❖ Carbohydrates: 20g
- ❖ Fat: 40g
- ❖ Sodium: 800mg
- ❖ Fiber: 4g

Conclude your meal with Moroccan Lamb Tagine with Green Olives and Carrots. This dish promises a delightful escape to the flavors of Morocco. Whether you're a connoisseur of global cuisines or seeking a new taste adventure, this recipe from our Slow Cooker Cookbook offers a delicious and aromatic experience, making it a perfect way to indulge in the rich tapestry of Moroccan cooking.

Recipe 03: Lamb Stew

Delve into the hearty and comforting flavors of "Lamb Stew with Potatoes and Carrot," a classic dish from our Slow Cooker Cookbook. This recipe combines tender chunks of lamb, earthy potatoes, and sweet carrots, all simmered in a rich and savory broth. Perfect for those seeking a nourishing and satisfying meal, it's a culinary embrace that promises warmth and fulfillment with every spoonful, ideal for a cozy night.

Servings: 1

Cook Time: 8 hours

Prepping Time: 15 minutes

Difficulty: Easy

Ingredients:

- ✓ 1/2 lb lamb, cut into chunks
- ✓ 1 large potato, cubed
- ✓ 1 carrot, sliced
- ✓ 1 onion, chopped
- ✓ 2 cloves garlic, minced
- ✓ 2 cups beef broth
- ✓ 1 teaspoon rosemary
- ✓ Salt and pepper to taste
- ✓ Fresh parsley for garnish

Step-by-Step Preparation:

1. Place lamb, potato, carrot, onion, and garlic in the slow cooker.
2. Pour beef broth over the ingredients.
3. Season with rosemary, salt, and pepper.
4. Cook on low for 8 hours, until lamb is tender and vegetables are soft.
5. Adjust seasoning if needed.
6. Serve hot, garnished with fresh parsley.

Nutritional Facts: (Per serving)

- ❖ Calories: 500
- ❖ Protein: 35g
- ❖ Carbohydrates: 40g
- ❖ Fat: 20g
- ❖ Sodium: 700mg
- ❖ Fiber: 5g

Conclude your meal with Lamb Stew with Potatoes and Carrot, a dish that is a testament to the simple pleasures of home cooking. Whether you're a fan of traditional stews or exploring the comforting recipes of our Slow Cooker Cookbook, this dish offers a delicious way to enjoy the rich flavors of lamb, making it a perfect choice for a hearty and satisfying dining experience.

Recipe 04: Hungarian Hot Goulash

Embark on a culinary expedition to Eastern Europe with "Hungarian Hot Goulash Soup," a fiery and flavorful dish from our Slow Cooker Cookbook. This authentic recipe captures the essence of Hungarian cuisine, combining tender beef, robust paprika, and a medley of vegetables in a rich and spicy broth. Perfect for those seeking to warm up with a bowl of hearty soup, it offers a comforting and satisfying experience, promising to transport your taste buds straight to the heart of Hungary.

Servings: 1

Cook Time: 8 hours

Prepping Time: 20 minutes

Difficulty: Easy

Ingredients:

- ✓ 1/2 lb beef chuck, cut into cubes
- ✓ 1 potato, cubed
- ✓ 1 carrot, sliced
- ✓ 1 onion, chopped
- ✓ 2 cloves garlic, minced
- ✓ 2 tablespoons paprika
- ✓ 1 teaspoon caraway seeds
- ✓ 4 cups beef broth
- ✓ Salt and pepper to taste
- ✓ Sour cream for serving

Step-by-Step Preparation:

1. Place beef, potato, carrot, onion, and garlic in the slow cooker.
2. Sprinkle with paprika and caraway seeds.
3. Pour beef broth over the mixture and season with salt and pepper.
4. Cook on low for 8 hours until beef is tender.
5. Serve hot, topped with a dollop of sour cream.

Nutritional Facts: (Per serving)

- ❖ Calories: 600
- ❖ Protein: 40g
- ❖ Carbohydrates: 40g
- ❖ Fat: 30g
- ❖ Sodium: 800mg
- ❖ Fiber: 6g

Conclude your meal with Hungarian Hot Goulash Soup, a dish that embodies the warmth and richness of traditional Hungarian fare. Whether you're a lover of hearty soups or exploring the diverse flavors of the world, this recipe from our Slow Cooker Cookbook offers a delectable way to enjoy the classic taste of goulash, ensuring a memorable and cozy dining experience.

Recipe 05: Mexican Beef Birria

Immerse yourself in the bold and vibrant flavors of "Mexican Beef Birria," an irresistible dish from our Slow Cooker Cookbook. This traditional recipe combines tender beef marinated in a rich, spicy sauce, creating an intensely flavorful and aromatic meal. Perfect for those who crave the authentic taste of Mexican cuisine, it's a culinary delight that promises to satisfy your hunger and spice up your dining experience.

Servings: 1

Prepping Time: 20 minutes

Cook Time: 8 hours

Difficulty: Medium

Ingredients:

- ✓ 1/2 lb beef chuck, cut into chunks
- ✓ 2 dried guajillo chiles, seeded
- ✓ 2 dried ancho chiles, seeded
- ✓ 1/2 onion, chopped
- ✓ 2 cloves garlic
- ✓ 1 teaspoon cumin
- ✓ 1 teaspoon oregano
- ✓ 1/2 teaspoon ground cloves
- ✓ 2 cups beef broth
- ✓ Salt to taste
- ✓ Fresh cilantro for garnish
- ✓ Lime wedges for serving

Step-by-Step Preparation:

1. Rehydrate guajillo and ancho chiles in hot water until soft.
2. Blend chiles, onion, garlic, cumin, oregano, cloves, and a bit of beef broth to make a smooth sauce.
3. Season beef chunks with salt and coat them in the chile sauce.
4. Place the beef in the slow cooker and pour the remaining beef broth over it.
5. Cook on low for 8 hours until beef is tender and pulls apart quickly.
6. Serve garnished with fresh cilantro and lime wedges on the side.

Nutritional Facts: (Per serving)

- ❖ Calories: 450
- ❖ Protein: 35g
- ❖ Carbohydrates: 20g
- ❖ Fat: 25g
- ❖ Sodium: 700mg
- ❖ Fiber: 4g

Conclude your meal with Mexican Beef Birria, a dish that feeds the body and warms the soul. Whether you're celebrating a special occasion or simply indulging in the rich tapestry of Mexican culinary traditions, this recipe from our Slow Cooker Cookbook offers a flavorful journey, making every bite a testament to the art of slow cooking and the robust flavors of Mexico.

Recipe 06: Beef Stew

Savor the rich and hearty flavors of "Beef Stewed with Potatoes in Tomato Sauce," a comforting dish from our Slow Cooker Cookbook. This recipe combines tender, slow-cooked Beef and soft potatoes in a flavorful tomato sauce, creating a simple yet deeply satisfying meal. Perfect for anyone seeking the warmth of home-cooked comfort food, it's a culinary hug that promises to delight your palate and nourish your soul with every spoonful.

Servings: 1

Cook Time: 8 hours

Prepping Time: 15 minutes

Difficulty: Easy

Ingredients:

- ✓ 1/2 lb beef chuck, cut into cubes
- ✓ 2 medium potatoes, cubed
- ✓ 1 cup tomato sauce
- ✓ 1/2 onion, chopped
- ✓ 1 clove garlic, minced
- ✓ 1 teaspoon dried thyme
- ✓ Salt and pepper to taste
- ✓ 2 cups beef broth
- ✓ Fresh parsley for garnish

Step-by-Step Preparation:

1. Season beef with salt and pepper and place in the slow cooker.
2. Add potatoes, onion, garlic, and thyme.
3. Pour tomato sauce and beef broth over the ingredients.
4. Cook on low for 8 hours, until Beef is tender and potatoes are soft.
5. Adjust seasoning if needed.
6. Serve hot, garnished with fresh parsley.

Nutritional Facts: (Per serving)

- ❖ Calories: 500
- ❖ Protein: 40g
- ❖ Carbohydrates: 45g
- ❖ Fat: 20g
- ❖ Sodium: 600mg
- ❖ Fiber: 6g

Conclude your dining experience with Beef Stewed with Potatoes in Tomato Sauce. This dish stands as a testament to the beauty of slow cooking. Whether you're seeking comfort on a chilly evening or a nutritious meal any day, this recipe from our Slow Cooker Cookbook delivers a mouthwatering blend of flavors and textures, ensuring a fulfilling and cozy dining experience.

Recipe 07: Mutton Korma

Indulge in the exquisite flavors of "Mutton Korma, Spicy Gravy with Tender Mutton Meat," a luxurious dish from our Slow Cooker Cookbook. This recipe brings to life the rich and aromatic essence of traditional korma with its blend of spices, yogurt, and tender mutton, slow-cooked to perfection. Ideal for those who appreciate the depth of Indian cuisine, it promises an opulent and comforting dining experience, making every bite a celebration of intricate flavors and succulent meat.

Servings: 1

Prepping Time: 20 minutes

Cook Time: 8 hours

Difficulty: Medium

Ingredients:

- ✓ 1/2 lb mutton, cut into pieces
- ✓ 1/2 cup yogurt
- ✓ 1 onion, finely sliced
- ✓ 2 cloves garlic, minced
- ✓ 1 inch ginger, minced
- ✓ 2 tablespoons korma spice blend
- ✓ 1 cup water
- ✓ Salt to taste
- ✓ 2 tablespoons ghee
- ✓ Fresh cilantro for garnish

Step-by-Step Preparation:

1. Marinate mutton in yogurt and korma spice blend for at least 1 hour.
2. In the slow cooker, sauté onion, garlic, and ginger in ghee until golden.
3. Add the marinated mutton and water. Season with salt.
4. Cook on low for 8 hours until the mutton is tender and the gravy is flavorful.
5. Garnish with fresh cilantro before serving.

Nutritional Facts: (Per serving)

- ❖ Calories: 600
- ❖ Protein: 50g
- ❖ Carbohydrates: 10g
- ❖ Fat: 40g
- ❖ Sodium: 500mg
- ❖ Fiber: 2g

Conclude your meal with Mutton Korma and Spicy Gravy with Tender Mutton Meat. This dish exemplifies the art of slow cooking and the richness of Indian spices. Whether it's a special occasion or a desire for a sumptuous meal, this recipe from our Slow Cooker Cookbook delivers an unforgettable culinary journey, ensuring a lavish and satisfying dining experience.

Recipe 08: Meat Osso Buco

Embark on a gourmet journey with "Ossobuco Served with Stewed Vegetables," a masterpiece from our Slow Cooker Cookbook. This dish showcases the Italian classic Ossobuco, featuring tender veal shanks slow-cooked to perfection, paired with a medley of beautifully stewed vegetables. It is ideal for connoisseurs seeking a sophisticated yet comforting meal; it offers a symphony of flavors and textures, promising a dining experience that's as nourishing as indulgent.

Servings: 1

Prepping Time: 20 minutes

Cook Time: 8 hours

Difficulty: Medium

Ingredients:

- ✓ 1 veal shank (Ossobuco)
- ✓ 1 carrot, diced
- ✓ 1 celery stalk, diced
- ✓ 1 onion, chopped
- ✓ 2 cloves garlic, minced
- ✓ 1 cup diced tomatoes
- ✓ 1/2 cup white wine
- ✓ 1/2 cup beef broth
- ✓ 1 teaspoon thyme
- ✓ Salt and pepper to taste
- ✓ Fresh parsley for garnish

Step-by-Step Preparation:

1. Season the veal shank with salt and pepper.
2. Combine carrot, celery, onion, and garlic in the slow cooker.
3. Place the veal shank on top of the vegetables.
4. Add diced tomatoes, white wine, beef broth, and thyme.
5. Cook on low for 8 hours until the meat is fall-off-the-bone tender.
6. Serve the Ossobuco with the stewed vegetables, garnished with fresh parsley.

Nutritional Facts: (Per serving)

- ❖ Calories: 550
- ❖ Protein: 60g
- ❖ Carbohydrates: 20g
- ❖ Fat: 20g
- ❖ Sodium: 600mg
- ❖ Fiber: 5g

Conclude your meal with Ossobuco Served with Stewed Vegetables. This dish not only satisfies the palate but also comforts the soul. Whether it's a special occasion or a desire for a luxurious home-cooked meal, this recipe from our Slow Cooker Cookbook delivers an exquisite blend of flavors, making it a memorable and heartwarming choice for any solo gourmet adventure.

Recipe 09: Beef Short Ribs

Immerse yourself in the rich and aromatic world of Korean cuisine with "Korean Beef Short Ribs Soup," a soulful dish from our Slow Cooker Cookbook. This delicacy combines tender beef short ribs with traditional Korean flavors, simmered to create a deeply satisfying soup. Perfect for anyone seeking comfort in a bowl, it promises a culinary experience that's both nourishing and flavorful, embodying the essence of Korean home cooking in every sip.

Servings: 1

Cook Time: 8 hours

Prepping Time: 20 minutes

Difficulty: Easy

Ingredients:

- ✓ 1/2 lb beef short ribs
- ✓ 4 cups water
- ✓ 1/2 onion, sliced
- ✓ 2 cloves garlic, minced
- ✓ 1 tablespoon soy sauce
- ✓ 1 teaspoon sesame oil
- ✓ 1/2 teaspoon red pepper flakes
- ✓ Salt to taste
- ✓ Green onions, sliced, for garnish
- ✓ Sesame seeds, for garnish

Step-by-Step Preparation:

1. Place beef short ribs in the slow cooker.
2. Add water, onion, garlic, soy sauce, sesame oil, and red pepper flakes.
3. Cook on low for 8 hours until ribs are tender.
4. Season with salt to taste.
5. Serve hot, garnished with sliced green onions and sesame seeds.

Nutritional Facts: (Per serving)

- ❖ Calories: 500
- ❖ Protein: 40g
- ❖ Carbohydrates: 5g
- ❖ Fat: 35g
- ❖ Sodium: 700mg
- ❖ Fiber: 1g

Conclude your dining experience with Korean Beef Short Ribs Soup, which brings warmth and comfort with its rich flavors and tender meat. Whether you're a fan of Korean cuisine or exploring new tastes, this recipe from our Slow Cooker Cookbook offers a delicious way to experience the depth and warmth of Korean cooking, making it a perfect choice for a cozy and satisfying meal.

Recipe 10: Lamb Shank

Savor the elegance of fine dining with "Lamb Shank in Red Wine Sauce Dressing with Potato and Broccoli," a sumptuous dish from our Slow Cooker Cookbook. This recipe marries the rich, fall-off-the-bone tenderness of lamb shank with the sophistication of a red wine sauce, accompanied by the wholesome goodness of potatoes and broccoli. It's ideal for those seeking a luxurious meal that comforts as much as it impresses; it's a culinary masterpiece that promises a perfect dining experience.

Servings: 1

Cook Time: 8 hours

Prepping Time: 20 minutes

Difficulty: Medium

Ingredients:

- ✓ 1 lamb shank
- ✓ 1 cup red wine
- ✓ 1 large potato, cubed
- ✓ 1 cup broccoli florets
- ✓ 1 onion, chopped
- ✓ 2 cloves garlic, minced
- ✓ 1 teaspoon rosemary
- ✓ 1 teaspoon thyme
- ✓ Salt and pepper to taste
- ✓ Olive oil for searing

Step-by-Step Preparation:

1. Sear the lamb shank in olive oil until browned on all sides.
2. Place the lamb shank, potato, broccoli, onion, and garlic in the slow cooker.
3. Pour red wine over the ingredients and season with rosemary, thyme, salt, and pepper.
4. Cook on low for 8 hours until the lamb is tender.
5. Serve the lamb shank with vegetables and red wine sauce.

Nutritional Facts: (Per serving)

- ❖ Calories: 650
- ❖ Protein: 48g
- ❖ Carbohydrates: 45g
- ❖ Fat: 25g
- ❖ Sodium: 750mg
- ❖ Fiber: 7g

Conclude your meal with Lamb Shank in Red Wine Sauce Dressing with Potato and Broccoli, a dish that encapsulates the essence of gourmet cooking. Whether it's a special occasion or a treat to yourself, this recipe from our Slow Cooker Cookbook delivers a symphony of flavors, ensuring a memorable and deeply satisfying culinary journey.

CHAPTER 03: POULTRY CHEF

Recipe 01: Chicken Cacciatore

Embark on a flavorful adventure with "Chicken Cacciatore with Sliced Capsicum," a rustic and hearty dish from our Slow Cooker Cookbook. This Italian classic combines succulent chicken with the sweet and vibrant flavors of capsicum, stewed in a rich tomato sauce with herbs and spices. Perfect for those seeking a comforting and aromatic meal, it's a simple yet sophisticated dish that satisfies your cravings for home-cooked excellence.

Servings: 1

Prepping Time: 15 minutes

Cook Time: 6 hours

Difficulty: Easy

Ingredients:

- ✓ 1 chicken breast, cut into pieces
- ✓ 1/2 cup sliced capsicum (bell peppers)
- ✓ 1/2 onion, sliced
- ✓ 2 cloves garlic, minced
- ✓ 1 can diced tomatoes
- ✓ 1 teaspoon dried oregano
- ✓ 1 teaspoon dried basil
- ✓ Salt and pepper to taste
- ✓ Olive oil for searing
- ✓ Fresh parsley for garnish

Step-by-Step Preparation:

1. Sear the chicken pieces in olive oil until browned.
2. Place the chicken, capsicum, onion, and garlic in the slow cooker.
3. Add diced tomatoes, oregano, basil, salt, and pepper.
4. Cook on low for 6 hours until chicken is tender.
5. Adjust seasoning to taste.
6. Serve garnished with fresh parsley.

Nutritional Facts: (Per serving)

- ❖ Calories: 350
- ❖ Protein: 28g
- ❖ Carbohydrates: 25g
- ❖ Fat: 15g
- ❖ Sodium: 500mg
- ❖ Fiber: 5g

Conclude your dining experience with Chicken Cacciatore with Sliced Capsicum. This dish brings the warmth and richness of Italian cooking to your table. Whether you're a seasoned chef or a novice in the kitchen, this recipe from our Slow Cooker Cookbook provides a delightful way to enjoy a classic favorite, making every meal a special occasion.

Recipe 02: Mussaman Curry

Immerse yourself in the complex flavors of "Chicken Mussaman Curry with Peanut and Raisin," a standout dish from our Slow Cooker Cookbook. This Thai-inspired curry melds the tender juiciness of chicken with the nutty depth of peanuts and the sweet pop of raisins; all enveloped in a rich, spiced sauce. Ideal for those craving an exotic and comforting dish, it promises a culinary adventure that's as rewarding as delicious.

Servings: 1

Prepping Time: 20 minutes

Cook Time: 6 hours

Difficulty: Medium

Ingredients:

- ✓ 1 chicken breast, cut into chunks
- ✓ 1/4 cup peanuts
- ✓ 1/4 cup raisins
- ✓ 1/2 can of coconut milk
- ✓ 2 tablespoons Mussaman curry paste
- ✓ 1/2 onion, chopped
- ✓ 1 potato, cubed
- ✓ 1 carrot, sliced
- ✓ Salt to taste
- ✓ Fresh cilantro for garnish

Step-by-Step Preparation:

1. Combine chicken, coconut milk, and curry paste in the slow cooker.
2. Add onion, potato, carrot, peanuts, and raisins.
3. Season with salt and mix well.
4. Cook on low for 6 hours, until chicken is tender and vegetables are soft.
5. Adjust seasoning if necessary.
6. Serve garnished with fresh cilantro.

Nutritional Facts: (Per serving)

- ❖ Calories: 500
- ❖ Protein: 30g
- ❖ Carbohydrates: 40g
- ❖ Fat: 25g
- ❖ Sodium: 300mg
- ❖ Fiber: 5g

Conclude your meal with Chicken Mussaman Curry with Peanuts and Raisins, a dish that effortlessly combines the savory with the sweet for a uniquely satisfying taste. Whether you're a fan of Thai cuisine or exploring new flavors, this recipe from our Slow Cooker Cookbook offers a delightful and hearty meal, ensuring a memorable dining experience.

Recipe 03: Tikka Masala

Embark on a flavorful journey with "Chicken Tikka Masala Spicy Curry," a beloved dish from our Slow Cooker Cookbook. This recipe brings the aromatic magic of Indian cuisine to your kitchen, featuring succulent chicken pieces enveloped in a creamy, spiced tomato sauce. Perfect for those who crave the vibrant tastes of India, it promises a dining experience that's both richly satisfying and delightfully intense, capturing the essence of traditional flavors with a modern twist.

Servings: 1

Prepping Time: 20 minutes

Cook Time: 6 hours

Difficulty: Medium

Ingredients:

- ✓ 1 chicken breast, cubed
- ✓ 1/2 cup plain yogurt
- ✓ 1 cup tomato sauce
- ✓ 2 tablespoons tikka masala spice blend
- ✓ 1/2 onion, finely chopped
- ✓ 2 cloves garlic, minced
- ✓ 1 teaspoon ginger, grated
- ✓ 1/4 cup heavy cream
- ✓ Salt to taste
- ✓ Fresh cilantro for garnish

Step-by-Step Preparation:

1. Marinate chicken in yogurt and tikka masala spice blend for 1 hour.
2. Place marinated chicken, onion, garlic, and ginger in the slow cooker.
3. Pour tomato sauce over the ingredients.
4. Cook on low for 6 hours, until chicken is tender.
5. Stir in heavy cream during the last 15 minutes of cooking.
6. Season with salt to taste.
7. Serve garnished with fresh cilantro.

Nutritional Facts: (Per serving)

- ❖ Calories: 450
- ❖ Protein: 30g
- ❖ Carbohydrates: 20g
- ❖ Fat: 25g
- ❖ Sodium: 800mg
- ❖ Fiber: 3g

Conclude your meal with Chicken Tikka Masala Spicy Curry, a dish that's as comforting as it is bold. Whether you're a longtime fan of Indian cuisine or exploring new culinary horizons, this recipe from our Slow Cooker Cookbook offers a perfect blend of warmth, spice, and flavor, ensuring a memorable and satisfying culinary adventure.

Recipe 04: Chicken Marsala

Indulge in the classic elegance of "Chicken Marsala," a distinguished recipe from our Slow Cooker Cookbook. This dish pairs the tender juiciness of chicken with the rich, aromatic flavors of Marsala wine and mushrooms, creating a harmonious blend that's both sophisticated and comforting. Ideal for those seeking a gourmet meal with minimal fuss, it offers a taste of Italian finesse that's sure to impress, making every dining experience a special occasion.

Servings: 1

Prepping Time: 15 minutes

Cook Time: 5 hours

Difficulty: Easy

Ingredients:

- ✓ 1 chicken breast, pounded to even thickness
- ✓ 1/2 cup Marsala wine
- ✓ 1/2 cup chicken broth
- ✓ 1/2 cup sliced mushrooms
- ✓ 1 small onion, thinly sliced
- ✓ 2 cloves garlic, minced
- ✓ Salt and pepper to taste
- ✓ 2 tablespoons flour, for dredging
- ✓ Olive oil, for searing
- ✓ Fresh parsley, for garnish

Step-by-Step Preparation:

1. Season the chicken with salt and pepper, then dredge in flour.
2. Sear in olive oil until golden, then place in the slow cooker.
3. Add Marsala wine, chicken broth, mushrooms, onion, and garlic.
4. Cook on low for 5 hours, until chicken is tender.
5. Adjust seasoning to taste.
6. Serve garnished with fresh parsley.

Nutritional Facts: (Per serving)

- ❖ Calories: 400
- ❖ Protein: 30g
- ❖ Carbohydrates: 15g
- ❖ Fat: 20g
- ❖ Sodium: 300mg
- ❖ Fiber: 1g

Conclude your meal with Chicken Marsala, a dish that perfectly encapsulates the joy of fine dining at home. Whether you're a seasoned chef or a culinary novice, this recipe from our Slow Cooker Cookbook provides a simple yet elegant way to enjoy the timeless combination of chicken and Marsala, ensuring a delightful and flavorful dining experience.

Recipe 05: Chicken and Apricot Tajine

Embark on a culinary journey to North Africa with "Chicken and Apricot Tajine Served Over Couscous," a vibrant dish from our Slow Cooker Cookbook. This exquisite recipe infuses tender chicken with the sweet tang of apricots and the aromatic warmth of ginger, cinnamon, chili, and honey, all slow-cooked to perfection. Ideal for those seeking to explore the rich tapestry of Moroccan flavors, it promises a dining experience that's both exotic and comforting, with each spoonful a celebration of culture and taste.

Servings: 1

Prepping Time: 20 minutes

Cook Time: 6 hours

Difficulty: Medium

Ingredients:

- ✓ 1 chicken breast, cut into pieces
- ✓ 1/4 cup dried apricots, chopped
- ✓ 1/2 cup couscous
- ✓ 1/2 teaspoon ground ginger
- ✓ 1/2 teaspoon ground cinnamon
- ✓ A pinch of chili powder
- ✓ 1 tablespoon honey
- ✓ 1 cup chicken broth
- ✓ Salt and pepper to taste
- ✓ Fresh cilantro, for garnish

Step-by-Step Preparation:

1. Combine chicken, apricots, ginger, cinnamon, chili powder, and honey in the slow cooker.
2. Pour chicken broth over the mixture, ensuring ingredients are well coated.
3. Cook on low for 6 hours, until chicken is tender and flavors meld.
4. Prepare couscous according to package instructions.
5. Serve chicken and apricot tajine over couscous, garnished with fresh cilantro.

Nutritional Facts: (Per serving)

- ❖ Calories: 500
- ❖ Protein: 35g
- ❖ Carbohydrates: 75g
- ❖ Fat: 5g
- ❖ Sodium: 300mg
- ❖ Fiber: 4g

Conclude your meal with Chicken and Apricot Tajine Served Over Couscous. This dish not only satiates your hunger but also transports you to the heart of Moroccan cuisine. Whether you're a lover of global flavors or seeking a new culinary adventure, this recipe from our Slow Cooker Cookbook offers a perfect blend of spice, sweetness, and satisfaction, making every bite a memorable experience.

Recipe 06: Chicken Fricassee

Indulge in the comforting embrace of "Chicken Fricassee with Vegetables and Mushrooms in White Wine," a refined dish from our Slow Cooker Cookbook. This culinary delight features tender chicken bathed in a creamy white wine sauce, alongside a medley of hearty vegetables and earthy mushrooms. Ideal for those seeking a sophisticated yet comforting meal, it offers a perfect blend of flavors and textures, promising a dining experience that's both nourishing and elegantly satisfying.

Servings: 1

Cook Time: 6 hours

Prepping Time: 20 minutes

Difficulty: Medium

Ingredients:

- ✓ 1 chicken breast, cubed
- ✓ 1/2 cup mixed vegetables (carrots, peas, beans)
- ✓ 1/2 cup mushrooms, sliced
- ✓ 1/2 onion, chopped
- ✓ 2 cloves garlic, minced
- ✓ 1/2 cup white wine
- ✓ 1/2 cup chicken broth
- ✓ 2 tablespoons heavy cream
- ✓ Salt and pepper to taste
- ✓ Fresh parsley, for garnish

Step-by-Step Preparation:

1. Place chicken, vegetables, mushrooms, onion, and garlic in the slow cooker.
2. Pour white wine and chicken broth over the ingredients.
3. Cook on low for 6 hours, until chicken is tender.
4. Stir in heavy cream during the last 15 minutes of cooking.
5. Season with salt and pepper to taste.
6. Serve garnished with fresh parsley.

Nutritional Facts: (Per serving)

- ❖ Calories: 450
- ❖ Protein: 30g
- ❖ Carbohydrates: 15g
- ❖ Fat: 20g
- ❖ Sodium: 300mg
- ❖ Fiber: 3g

Conclude your meal with Chicken Fricassee with Vegetables and Mushrooms in White Wine, a dish that effortlessly marries rustic charm with culinary finesse. Whether you're dining alone or entertaining guests, this recipe from our Slow Cooker Cookbook delivers a heartwarming and flavorful feast, ensuring a memorable and satisfying dining experience.

Recipe 07: Chicken Pasta

Dive into the sweet and tangy world of "Honey Mustard Chicken Pasta with Peppers," a delectable dish from our Slow Cooker Cookbook. This recipe combines the comforting taste of pasta, the succulent richness of chicken, and the vibrant flavors of peppers, all unified by a luscious honey mustard sauce. Perfect for those craving a hearty and flavorful meal, it promises a delightful fusion of tastes sure to please any palate.

Servings: 1

Prepping Time: 15 minutes

Cook Time: 4 hours

Difficulty: Easy

Ingredients:

- ✓ 1 chicken breast, cut into pieces
- ✓ 1/2 cup pasta, uncooked
- ✓ 1/4 cup honey
- ✓ 1/4 cup mustard
- ✓ 1/2 bell pepper, sliced
- ✓ 1/2 onion, sliced
- ✓ 1 garlic clove, minced
- ✓ Salt and pepper to taste
- ✓ Fresh herbs (parsley or basil) for garnish

Step-by-Step Preparation:

1. Place chicken pieces in the slow cooker.
2. Top with sliced bell pepper, onion, and minced garlic.
3. Mix honey and mustard in a bowl, then pour over the chicken and vegetables.
4. Season with salt and pepper.
5. Cook on low for 4 hours until chicken is tender.
6. Cook pasta according to package instructions and add to the slow cooker in the last 30 minutes.
7. Serve garnished with fresh herbs.

Nutritional Facts: (Per serving)

- ❖ Calories: 550
- ❖ Protein: 35g
- ❖ Carbohydrates: 70g
- ❖ Fat: 15g
- ❖ Sodium: 300mg
- ❖ Fiber: 3g

Conclude your dining experience with Honey Mustard Chicken Pasta with Peppers, a dish that perfectly captures the essence of comfort food with a twist. Whether you're a culinary enthusiast or simply seeking a delicious and easy-to-prepare meal, this recipe from our Slow Cooker Cookbook offers a satisfying and flavorful option, making it a memorable highlight of any mealtime.

Recipe 08: Green Chicken Curry

Explore the vibrant flavors of Southeast Asia with "Green Chicken Curry," an irresistible dish from our Slow Cooker Cookbook. This recipe combines tender chicken pieces with the aromatic blend of green curry paste, coconut milk, and various fresh vegetables, creating a rich and spicy, comforting, exotic curry. Perfect for those seeking a culinary adventure, it offers a deliciously smooth and flavorful journey that will satisfy your craving for Thai cuisine.

Servings: 1

Prepping Time: 15 minutes

Cook Time: 4 hours

Difficulty: Easy

Ingredients:

- ✓ 1 chicken breast, cubed
- ✓ 1/2 cup coconut milk
- ✓ 2 tablespoons green curry paste
- ✓ 1/2 bell pepper, sliced
- ✓ 1/4 cup bamboo shoots
- ✓ 1/2 carrot, sliced
- ✓ 1/2 onion, sliced
- ✓ 1 tablespoon fish sauce
- ✓ 1 teaspoon sugar
- ✓ Basil leaves, for garnish

Step-by-Step Preparation:

1. Place chicken in the slow cooker.
2. Mix coconut milk and green curry paste and pour over chicken.
3. Add bell pepper, bamboo shoots, carrot, and onion.
4. Season with fish sauce and sugar.
5. Cook on low for 4 hours until chicken is tender and vegetables are cooked.
6. Garnish with basil leaves before serving.

Nutritional Facts: (Per serving)

- ❖ Calories: 400
- ❖ Protein: 30g
- ❖ Carbohydrates: 15g
- ❖ Fat: 25g
- ❖ Sodium: 600mg
- ❖ Fiber: 2g

Conclude your meal with Green Chicken Curry, a dish that embodies the essence of Thai cooking with its harmonious blend of flavors and textures. Whether you're a seasoned fan of Asian cuisine or exploring new tastes, this recipe from our Slow Cooker Cookbook delivers an authentic and satisfying experience, making it a perfect choice for any occasion.

Recipe 09: Asparagus Tagliatelle

Savor the essence of spring with "Asparagus Tagliatelle with Green Pesto, Tomatoes, and Chicken," a harmonious dish from our Slow Cooker Cookbook. This culinary creation combines the tender juiciness of chicken, the fresh snap of asparagus, and the juiciness of tomatoes, all brought together with a vibrant green pesto sauce. Ideal for those seeking a dish that's as colorful as it is flavorful, it promises a delightful blend of freshness and satisfaction, perfect for any solo gourmet adventure.

Servings: 1

Prepping Time: 15 minutes

Cook Time: 3 hours

Difficulty: Easy

Ingredients:

- ✓ 1/2 chicken breast, cut into pieces
- ✓ 1/2 cup tagliatelle pasta
- ✓ 1 cup asparagus, chopped
- ✓ 1/2 cup cherry tomatoes, halved
- ✓ 2 tablespoons green pesto
- ✓ Salt and pepper to taste
- ✓ Grated Parmesan cheese for garnish
- ✓ Fresh basil leaves for garnish

Step-by-Step Preparation:

1. Place chicken pieces in the slow cooker.
2. Add asparagus and cherry tomatoes on top.
3. Season with salt and pepper.
4. Cook on low for 3 hours until chicken is tender and vegetables are cooked.
5. Cook tagliatelle according to package directions.
6. Toss cooked pasta with the chicken and vegetable mixture and green pesto.
7. Serve garnished with Parmesan cheese and fresh basil.

Nutritional Facts: (Per serving)

- ❖ Calories: 500
- ❖ Protein: 35g
- ❖ Carbohydrates: 50g
- ❖ Fat: 18g
- ❖ Sodium: 320mg
- ❖ Fiber: 4g

Conclude your meal with Asparagus Tagliatelle with Green Pesto, Tomatoes, and Chicken. This dish captures the freshness of the season with every bite. Whether you're seeking a light yet fulfilling meal or a new way to enjoy your pasta, this recipe from our Slow Cooker Cookbook delivers a beautifully balanced and deliciously inviting experience, making it a perfect choice for any occasion.

Recipe 10: Butter Chicken Curry

Embark on a culinary voyage to the heart of Indian cuisine with "Butter Chicken Curry," a luxuriously creamy and aromatic dish from our Slow Cooker Cookbook. This recipe skillfully blends tender chicken pieces with a rich, spiced tomato and cream sauce, offering a profoundly satisfying and flavorful experience. Perfect for those seeking comfort in a bowl, it promises a decadent treat that's as soul-warming as delicious, capturing the essence of traditional Indian flavors with every bite.

Servings: 1

Prepping Time: 15 minutes

Cook Time: 4 hours

Difficulty: Easy

Ingredients:

- ✓ 1 chicken breast, cubed
- ✓ 1/2 cup tomato sauce
- ✓ 1/4 cup heavy cream
- ✓ 2 tablespoons butter
- ✓ 1 tablespoon garam masala
- ✓ 1 teaspoon turmeric
- ✓ 1 teaspoon cumin
- ✓ 1/2 teaspoon chili powder
- ✓ Salt to taste
- ✓ Fresh cilantro for garnish

Step-by-Step Preparation:

1. Place chicken cubes in the slow cooker.
2. Mix tomato sauce, heavy cream, butter, and spices in a bowl. Pour over the chicken.
3. Cook on low for 4 hours until chicken is tender and sauce thickens.
4. Adjust salt to taste.
5. Serve hot, garnished with fresh cilantro.

Nutritional Facts: (Per serving)

- ❖ Calories: 550
- ❖ Protein: 30g
- ❖ Carbohydrates: 8g
- ❖ Fat: 44g
- ❖ Sodium: 700mg
- ❖ Fiber: 2g

Conclude your meal with Butter Chicken Curry, a dish that stands as a testament to the rich and complex beauty of Indian cooking. Whether you're a seasoned fan or new to Indian cuisine, this recipe from our Slow Cooker Cookbook offers an effortlessly elegant way to enjoy a classic favorite, ensuring a memorable and comforting dining experience.

CHAPTER 04: VEGGIE VARIETIES

Recipe 01: Glazed Carrot With Fresh Basil

Delight in the simplicity and elegance of "Glazed Carrot with Fresh Basil," a vibrant dish from our Slow Cooker Cookbook. This recipe transforms humble carrots into a gourmet side dish, glazing them in a sweet buttery sauce enhanced with the freshness of basil. Ideal for those seeking to elevate their meal with a touch of sophistication, it offers a delicious harmony of flavors that beautifully complements any main course, promising a light yet memorable culinary experience.

Servings: 1

Prepping Time: 10 minutes

Cook Time: 3 hours

Difficulty: Easy

Ingredients:

- ✓ 1 cup carrots, sliced
- ✓ 2 tablespoons butter
- ✓ 1 tablespoon brown sugar
- ✓ Salt to taste
- ✓ Fresh basil leaves for garnish

Step-by-Step Preparation:

1. Place sliced carrots in the slow cooker.
2. Dot with butter and sprinkle brown sugar over the top.
3. Season with salt.
4. Cook on low for 3 hours until carrots are tender and glazed.
5. Garnish with fresh basil leaves before serving.

Nutritional Facts: (Per serving)

- ❖ Calories: 250
- ❖ Protein: 1g
- ❖ Carbohydrates: 20g
- ❖ Fat: 18g
- ❖ Sodium: 200mg
- ❖ Fiber: 3g

Conclude your dining experience with Glazed Carrots with Fresh Basil. This dish showcases the beauty of simple ingredients transformed through slow cooking. Whether you're hosting a dinner party or enjoying a quiet meal at home, this recipe from our Slow Cooker Cookbook provides a delightful way to enjoy carrots, making every bite a celebration of flavor and freshness.

Recipe 02: Cauliflower Stew With Curry

Embark on a flavorful journey with "Cauliflower Stew with Curry," a fragrant dish from our Slow Cooker Cookbook. This recipe celebrates the versatility of cauliflower, simmering it in a rich blend of aromatic spices that infuse warmth and depth into every bite. Perfect for those seeking a comforting yet adventurous meal, it promises a delectable fusion of flavors that's both nourishing and profoundly satisfying, making it a standout choice for any culinary explorer.

Servings: 1

Prepping Time: 15 minutes

Cook Time: 6 hours

Difficulty: Easy

Ingredients:

- ✓ 1 cup cauliflower florets
- ✓ 1/2 teaspoon curry powder
- ✓ 1/2 teaspoon cumin
- ✓ 1/2 teaspoon turmeric
- ✓ 1/4 teaspoon chili powder
- ✓ 1 cup vegetable broth
- ✓ Salt to taste
- ✓ Fresh cilantro for garnish

Step-by-Step Preparation:

1. Place cauliflower florets in the slow cooker.
2. Sprinkle with curry powder, cumin, turmeric, and chili powder.
3. Pour vegetable broth over the spices and cauliflower.
4. Season with salt.
5. Cook on low for 6 hours until cauliflower is tender and flavors meld.
6. Garnish with fresh cilantro before serving.

Nutritional Facts: (Per serving)

- ❖ Calories: 100
- ❖ Protein: 3g
- ❖ Carbohydrates: 10g
- ❖ Fat: 5g
- ❖ Sodium: 300mg
- ❖ Fiber: 4g

Conclude your meal with Cauliflower Stew with Curry, Cumin, Turmeric, and Other Spices. This dish warms the body and delights the senses. Whether you're a vegetarian or simply a lover of rich, spice-forward cuisine, this recipe from our Slow Cooker Cookbook delivers a comforting and aromatic dining experience, ensuring a memorable and healthful feast.

Recipe 03: Mushrooms With White Wine

Dive into the exquisite simplicity of "Mushrooms Cooked with White Wine," a sumptuous dish from our Slow Cooker Cookbook. This recipe elevates the humble mushroom to new heights, bathing it in the delicate flavors of white wine, herbs, and garlic. Perfect for those seeking a gourmet side dish or a vegetarian delight, it offers a rich and aromatic taste experience that's both refined and effortlessly elegant, promising to enhance any meal with its sophisticated charm.

Servings: 1

Prepping Time: 10 minutes

Cook Time: 2 hours

Difficulty: Easy

Ingredients:

- ✓ 1 cup mushrooms, sliced
- ✓ 1/2 cup white wine
- ✓ 1 garlic clove, minced
- ✓ 1 tablespoon olive oil
- ✓ Salt and pepper to taste
- ✓ Fresh herbs (thyme or parsley) for garnish

Step-by-Step Preparation:

1. Place mushrooms in the slow cooker.
2. Add minced garlic and olive oil.
3. Pour white wine over the mushrooms.
4. Season with salt and pepper.
5. Cook on low for 2 hours until mushrooms are tender and flavorful.
6. Garnish with fresh herbs before serving.

Nutritional Facts: (Per serving)

- ❖ Calories: 150
- ❖ Protein: 3g
- ❖ Carbohydrates: 6g
- ❖ Fat: 10g
- ❖ Sodium: 200mg
- ❖ Fiber: 1g

Conclude your dining experience with Mushrooms Cooked with White Wine, a dish that showcases the beauty of simplicity in cooking. Whether you're a mushroom lover or a connoisseur of delicate flavors, this recipe from our Slow Cooker Cookbook delivers a delightful and aromatic accompaniment to any main course, ensuring a memorable and tasteful addition to your culinary repertoire.

Recipe 04: Mediterranean Vegetable Stew

Embark on a culinary journey to the sunny Mediterranean with "Mediterranean Vegetable Stew," a vibrant dish from our Slow Cooker Cookbook. This recipe celebrates the garden's bounty, combining a variety of fresh vegetables with aromatic herbs and spices, all simmered to create a hearty and healthy stew. Ideal for those seeking a flavorful yet nutritious meal, it offers a delicious way to enjoy the essence of Mediterranean cuisine, promising a comforting and satisfying dining experience with every spoonful.

Servings: 1

Cook Time: 6 hours

Prepping Time: 15 minutes

Difficulty: Easy

Ingredients:

- ✓ 1/2 cup zucchini, chopped
- ✓ 1/2 cup eggplant, chopped
- ✓ 1/2 cup bell peppers, chopped
- ✓ 1/4 cup onions, chopped
- ✓ 2 cloves garlic, minced
- ✓ 1 cup diced tomatoes
- ✓ 1 teaspoon dried oregano
- ✓ 1 teaspoon dried basil
- ✓ Salt and pepper to taste
- ✓ Fresh parsley for garnish

Step-by-Step Preparation:

1. Place zucchini, eggplant, bell peppers, onions, and garlic in the slow cooker.
2. Add diced tomatoes and sprinkle with oregano and basil.
3. Season with salt and pepper.
4. Cook on low for 6 hours until vegetables are tender and flavors meld.
5. Adjust seasoning if necessary.
6. Serve hot, garnished with fresh parsley.

Nutritional Facts: (Per serving)

- ❖ Calories: 200
- ❖ Protein: 6g
- ❖ Carbohydrates: 30g
- ❖ Fat: 5g
- ❖ Sodium: 300mg
- ❖ Fiber: 8g

Conclude your meal with Mediterranean Vegetable Stew, a dish that nourishes the body and delights the senses. Whether embracing a plant-based lifestyle or simply seeking a taste of the Mediterranean, this recipe from our Slow Cooker Cookbook provides a warm, flavorful, and healthful choice, ensuring a delightful and fulfilling culinary voyage.

Recipe 05: Pasta With Broccoli & Edamame

Immerse yourself in the comforting embrace of "Pasta with Broccoli, Edamame, and Creamy Sauce," a heartwarming dish from our Slow Cooker Cookbook. This delightful recipe pairs the tender crunch of broccoli and the subtle sweetness of edamame with the silky richness of a creamy sauce; all enrobed in perfectly cooked pasta. Ideal for those seeking a nourishing and indulgently satisfying meal, it promises a harmonious blend of flavors and textures, making every bite a testament to the joys of simple, wholesome ingredients.

Servings: 1

Prepping Time: 15 minutes

Cook Time: 3 hours

Difficulty: Easy

Ingredients:

- ✓ 1/2 cup pasta
- ✓ 1/2 cup broccoli florets
- ✓ 1/2 cup shelled edamame
- ✓ 1/2 cup heavy cream
- ✓ 1 garlic clove, minced
- ✓ Salt and pepper to taste
- ✓ Grated Parmesan cheese for garnish

Step-by-Step Preparation:

1. Place broccoli and edamame in the slow cooker.
2. Add minced garlic and pour heavy cream over the vegetables. Season with salt and pepper.
3. Cook on low for 3 hours until vegetables are tender.
4. Cook pasta according to package directions.
5. Mix the cooked pasta with the creamy vegetable sauce.
6. Serve garnished with grated Parmesan cheese.

Nutritional Facts: (Per serving)

- ❖ Calories: 480
- ❖ Protein: 18g
- ❖ Carbohydrates: 45g
- ❖ Fat: 26g
- ❖ Sodium: 320mg
- ❖ Fiber: 6g

Conclude your meal with Pasta with Broccoli, Edamame, and Creamy Sauce. This dish celebrates the beauty of combining simple ingredients to create something extraordinary. Whether you're seeking comfort on a chilly evening or a quick yet satisfying meal, this recipe from our Slow Cooker Cookbook offers a delicious and easy way to enjoy the flavors of home, ensuring a delightful dining experience.

Recipe 06: Caramelized Onion Dip

Indulge in the rich, savory flavors of "Caramelized Onion Dip," a delectable creation from our Slow Cooker Cookbook. This recipe transforms simple onions into a lusciously sweet and spicy dip, slow-cooked to perfection, creating a depth of complex and comforting flavor. Ideal for gatherings or a solo treat, it promises to be the star of any snack table, offering a creamy, indulgent experience that's as addictive as it is satisfying.

Servings: 1

Prepping Time: 10 minutes

Cook Time: 8 hours

Difficulty: Easy

Ingredients:

- ✓ 2 large onions, thinly sliced
- ✓ 1 tablespoon butter
- ✓ 1 cup sour cream
- ✓ 1/4 cup mayonnaise
- ✓ Salt and pepper to taste
- ✓ Chopped chives for garnish

Step-by-Step Preparation:

1. Place sliced onions and butter in the slow cooker.
2. Cook on low for 8 hours until onions are deeply caramelized.
3. Allow onions to cool, then mix with sour cream and mayonnaise.
4. Season with salt and pepper.
5. Chill in the refrigerator for 1 hour before serving.
6. Garnish with chopped chives.

Nutritional Facts: (Per serving)

- ❖ Calories: 600
- ❖ Protein: 5g
- ❖ Carbohydrates: 20g
- ❖ Fat: 55g
- ❖ Sodium: 300mg
- ❖ Fiber: 2g

Conclude your dining experience with Caramelized Onion Dip. This dish effortlessly combines the joy of cooking with the pleasure of tasting. Whether entertaining guests or treating yourself, this recipe from our Slow Cooker Cookbook delivers a sophisticated and irresistible flavor, making it a perfect choice for any occasion.

Recipe 07: Aloo Gobi With Cauliflower & Potato

Embark on a flavorful journey to the heart of Indian cuisine with "Aloo Gobi with Cauliflower and Potato," a classic dish from our Slow Cooker Cookbook. This beloved recipe combines the earthy comfort of potatoes with the subtle, nutty taste of cauliflower, all seasoned with a rich tapestry of spices. Ideal for those seeking a deliciously aromatic and vegan-friendly meal, it promises a comforting, hearty experience that captures the essence of traditional Indian home cooking in every bite.

Servings: 1

Cook Time: 6 hours

Prepping Time: 15 minutes

Difficulty: Easy

Ingredients:

- ✓ 1 cup cauliflower florets
- ✓ 1 cup diced potatoes
- ✓ 1/2 cup diced tomatoes
- ✓ 1/2 onion, finely chopped
- ✓ 2 cloves garlic, minced
- ✓ 1 teaspoon turmeric
- ✓ 1 teaspoon cumin
- ✓ 1/2 teaspoon garam masala
- ✓ Salt and pepper to taste
- ✓ Fresh cilantro for garnish

Step-by-Step Preparation:

1. Place cauliflower, potatoes, tomatoes, onion, and garlic in the slow cooker.
2. Sprinkle with turmeric, cumin, and garam masala.
3. Season with salt and pepper.
4. Cook on low for 6 hours until vegetables are tender and flavors meld.
5. Adjust seasoning if necessary.
6. Garnish with fresh cilantro before serving.

Nutritional Facts: (Per serving)

- ❖ Calories: 200
- ❖ Protein: 5g
- ❖ Carbohydrates: 40g
- ❖ Fat: 1g
- ❖ Sodium: 200mg
- ❖ Fiber: 8g

Conclude your meal with Aloo Gobi with Cauliflower and Potato, a dish that nourishes the body and delights the palate. Whether you're a connoisseur of Indian cuisine or exploring new flavors, this recipe from our Slow Cooker Cookbook offers a simple yet profound way to enjoy the rich diversity of spices, making it a perfect choice for a comforting and satisfying dining experience.

Recipe 08: Stewed Vegetable Ratatouille

Delve into the rustic charm of "Stewed Vegetable Ratatouille," a vibrant dish from our Slow Cooker Cookbook. This recipe combines a medley of summer vegetables, each component stewed to perfection, creating a symphony of flavors and textures. Ideal for those seeking a wholesome and hearty meal, it captures the essence of Provencal cuisine, offering a comforting, nourishing experience that celebrates the garden's bounty with every spoonful.

Servings: 1

Cook Time: 5 hours

Prepping Time: 20 minutes

Difficulty: Easy

Ingredients:

- ✓ 1/2 cup eggplant, cubed
- ✓ 1/2 cup zucchini, cubed
- ✓ 1/2 cup bell pepper, chopped
- ✓ 1/2 cup tomatoes, diced
- ✓ 1/4 cup onion, chopped
- ✓ 2 cloves garlic, minced
- ✓ 1 teaspoon dried basil
- ✓ 1 teaspoon dried oregano
- ✓ Salt and pepper to taste
- ✓ Olive oil for drizzling
- ✓ Fresh basil for garnish

Step-by-Step Preparation:

1. Layer eggplant, zucchini, bell pepper, tomatoes, onion, and garlic in the slow cooker.
2. Sprinkle with dried basil, oregano, salt, and pepper.
3. Drizzle with olive oil.
4. Cook on low for 5 hours until vegetables are tender, and flavors are blended.
5. Adjust seasoning if necessary.
6. Serve garnished with fresh basil leaves.

Nutritional Facts: (Per serving)

- ❖ Calories: 150
- ❖ Protein: 4g
- ❖ Carbohydrates: 20g
- ❖ Fat: 7g
- ❖ Sodium: 200mg
- ❖ Fiber: 6g

Conclude your dining experience with Stewed Vegetable Ratatouille, a dish that embodies the warmth and simplicity of home cooking. Whether you're a lover of vegetables or seeking a light yet fulfilling meal, this recipe from our Slow Cooker Cookbook delivers a deliciously comforting and colorful feast, ensuring a delightful and healthful culinary journey.

Recipe 09: Creamed Spinach

Indulge in the creamy, comforting embrace of "Creamed Spinach with Onion and Garlic," a sumptuous dish from our Slow Cooker Cookbook. This recipe elevates the humble spinach into a luxurious side dish, combining it with the savory depth of onion and garlic, all enveloped in a velvety cream sauce. Ideal for those seeking to add a touch of elegance to their meals, it offers a rich and flavorful experience that's as satisfying as it is simple to prepare, making every bite a lush and aromatic delight.

Servings: 1

Prepping Time: 10 minutes

Cook Time: 2 hours

Difficulty: Easy

Ingredients:

- ✓ 1 cup fresh spinach
- ✓ 1/4 cup diced onion
- ✓ 1 garlic clove, minced
- ✓ 1/2 cup heavy cream
- ✓ Salt and pepper to taste
- ✓ Nutmeg, a pinch for flavor
- ✓ Grated Parmesan cheese for garnish

Step-by-Step Preparation:

1. Place spinach, onion, and garlic in the slow cooker.
2. Pour heavy cream over the vegetables. Season with salt, pepper, and a pinch of nutmeg.
3. Cook on low for 2 hours until the spinach is wilted and the sauce is thickened.
4. Stir well to ensure the spinach is evenly coated in the cream sauce.
5. Serve hot, garnished with grated Parmesan cheese.

Nutritional Facts: (Per serving)

- ❖ Calories: 300
- ❖ Protein: 5g
- ❖ Carbohydrates: 8g
- ❖ Fat: 28g
- ❖ Sodium: 200mg
- ❖ Fiber: 2g

Conclude your meal with Creamed Spinach with Onion and Garlic. This dish effortlessly combines spinach's nutritional goodness with a cream sauce indulgence. Whether as a side to a grand main course or a luxurious treat, this recipe from our Slow Cooker Cookbook delivers a comforting and decadent culinary experience, ensuring a memorable and flavorful addition to any dining occasion.

Recipe 10: Corn Zucchini and Bacon Chowder

Savor the comforting flavors of "Creamy Corn Zucchini and Bacon Chowder," a heartwarming dish from our Slow Cooker Cookbook. This recipe combines the sweetness of corn, the tender bite of zucchini, and the smoky richness of bacon in a creamy broth, creating a perfect blend of tastes and textures. Ideal for those seeking a cozy, nourishing meal, it offers a delightful comfort food experience, promising to warm your soul and satisfy your taste buds with its homely charm and depth of flavor.

Servings: 1

Cook Time: 4 hours

Prepping Time: 15 minutes

Difficulty: Easy

Ingredients:

- ✓ 1/2 cup corn kernels
- ✓ 1/2 cup chopped zucchini
- ✓ 2 slices bacon, chopped
- ✓ 1 cup chicken broth
- ✓ 1/2 cup heavy cream
- ✓ 1/4 onion, chopped
- ✓ 1 garlic clove, minced
- ✓ Salt and pepper to taste
- ✓ Fresh chives, for garnish

Step-by-Step Preparation:

1. Combine corn, zucchini, bacon, onion, and garlic in the slow cooker.
2. Pour chicken broth over the mixture.
3. Cook on low for 4 hours until vegetables are tender.
4. Stir in heavy cream during the last 30 minutes of cooking.
5. Season with salt and pepper to taste.
6. Serve hot, garnished with fresh chives.

Nutritional Facts: (Per serving)

- ❖ Calories: 450
- ❖ Protein: 10g
- ❖ Carbohydrates: 20g
- ❖ Fat: 36g
- ❖ Sodium: 750mg
- ❖ Fiber: 2g

Conclude your dining experience with Creamy Corn Zucchini and Bacon Chowder. This dish brings the essence of comfort to your table. Whether you're seeking a quick weeknight dinner or a hearty lunch, this recipe from our Slow Cooker Cookbook delivers a deliciously satisfying meal, ensuring a cozy and delightful culinary journey.

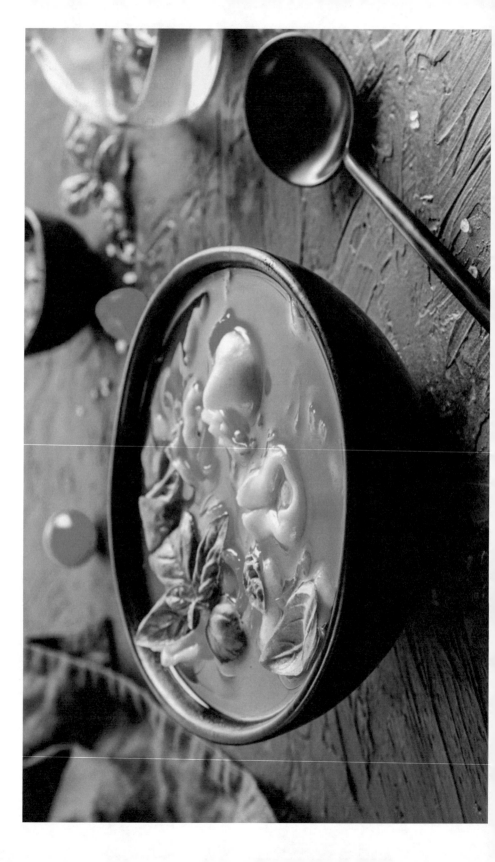

CHAPTER 05: SOUP SOLOS

Recipe 01: Tomato Tortellini Soup

Immerse yourself in the rich, comforting embrace of "Tomato Soup with Tortellini," a heartwarming dish from our Slow Cooker Cookbook. This recipe marries the robust flavors of ripe tomatoes with the delicate, cheese-filled tortellini, creating a harmonious, nourishing, and satisfying blend. Ideal for those seeking a soul-soothing meal, it promises a culinary experience that's as fulfilling as it is delicious, turning a classic soup into an elevated comfort food masterpiece with every spoonful.

Servings: 1

Cook Time: 6 hours

Prepping Time: 10 minutes

Difficulty: Easy

Ingredients:

- ✓ 1 cup canned crushed tomatoes
- ✓ 1 cup vegetable broth
- ✓ 1/2 cup cheese tortellini
- ✓ 1 garlic clove, minced
- ✓ 1/2 onion, chopped
- ✓ 1 teaspoon dried basil
- ✓ Salt and pepper to taste
- ✓ Grated Parmesan cheese for garnish
- ✓ Fresh basil for garnish

Step-by-Step Preparation:

1. Combine crushed tomatoes, vegetable broth, garlic, and onion in the slow cooker.
2. Season with dried basil, salt, and pepper.
3. Cook on low for 6 hours, allowing flavors to meld.
4. Add tortellini in the last 30 minutes of cooking.
5. Adjust seasoning if necessary.
6. Serve hot, garnished with grated Parmesan and fresh basil.

Nutritional Facts: (Per serving)

- ❖ Calories: 300
- ❖ Protein: 12g
- ❖ Carbohydrates: 40g
- ❖ Fat: 10g
- ❖ Sodium: 700mg
- ❖ Fiber: 5g

Conclude your meal with Tomato Soup with Tortellini, a dish that perfectly encapsulates the joy of simple, heartening cuisine. Whether you need a quick comfort meal or a delightful way to warm up, this recipe from our Slow Cooker Cookbook offers a timeless, flavorful solution, ensuring a comforting and satisfying dining experience.

Recipe 02: Beef Pho Bowl

Embark on a flavor journey with "Beef Pho - Noodle Soup with Sliced Beef," a classic dish from our Slow Cooker Cookbook. This Vietnamese culinary masterpiece combines silky rice noodles and tender slices of beef in a fragrant broth, steeped with spices and garnished with fresh herbs. Perfect for anyone craving a profoundly satisfying and aromatic meal, it's a testament to the power of simple ingredients coming together to create a comforting, soul-warming soup that's both nourishing and refreshing.

Servings: 1

Prepping Time: 15 minutes

Cook Time: 8 hours

Difficulty: Medium

Ingredients:

- ✓ 1/2 lb beef sirloin, thinly sliced
- ✓ 1 cup rice noodles
- ✓ 4 cups beef stock
- ✓ 1 small onion, charred
- ✓ 1 piece ginger, charred
- ✓ 3-star anise

- ✓ 1 cinnamon stick
- ✓ Fish sauce, to taste
- ✓ Salt, to taste
- ✓ Lime wedges, bean sprouts, basil, and jalapeños for garnish

Step-by-Step Preparation:

1. Combine beef stock, charred onion, ginger, star anise, and cinnamon stick in the slow cooker.
2. Season with fish sauce and salt, adjusting to taste.
3. Cook on low for 8 hours to develop the broth's flavors.
4. Prepare rice noodles as per package instructions.
5. Arrange noodles and sliced beef in a bowl, then ladle the hot broth.
6. To serve, garnish with lime wedges, bean sprouts, basil, and jalapeños.

Nutritional Facts: (Per serving)

- ❖ Calories: 510
- ❖ Protein: 35g
- ❖ Carbohydrates: 55g

- ❖ Fat: 15g
- ❖ Sodium: 850mg
- ❖ Fiber: 3g

Finish your meal with Beef Pho - Noodle Soup with Sliced Beef, a dish that captures the essence of Vietnamese cooking. Whether you're a seasoned pho lover or discovering its delights for the first time, this recipe from our Slow Cooker Cookbook offers an authentic taste of Vietnam, ensuring a culinary experience that's as enriching as it is delicious.

Recipe 03: Mushroom Cream Soup

Indulge in the rich, velvety embrace of "Mushroom Cream Soup," a gourmet delight from our Slow Cooker Cookbook. This exquisite recipe combines the earthy depth of mushrooms with the luxurious smoothness of cream, creating a comforting bowl of sophisticated and soul-soothing soup. Ideal for those seeking a sumptuous and warming meal, it offers a perfect blend of simplicity and elegance, promising a dining experience that's as indulgent as it is satisfying.

Servings: 1

Prepping Time: 10 minutes

Cook Time: 4 hours

Difficulty: Easy

Ingredients:

- ✓ 1 cup sliced mushrooms
- ✓ 1/2 cup heavy cream
- ✓ 1 cup vegetable broth
- ✓ 1/4 onion, finely chopped
- ✓ 1 garlic clove, minced
- ✓ Salt and pepper to taste
- ✓ Fresh thyme for garnish

Step-by-Step Preparation:

1. Place mushrooms, onion, and garlic in the slow cooker.
2. Pour vegetable broth over the mixture.
3. Cook on low for 4 hours until mushrooms are tender.
4. Blend the soup to the desired consistency, then stir in heavy cream.
5. Season with salt and pepper.
6. Serve hot, garnished with fresh thyme.

Nutritional Facts: (Per serving)

- ❖ Calories: 350
- ❖ Protein: 5g
- ❖ Carbohydrates: 8g
- ❖ Fat: 34g
- ❖ Sodium: 300mg
- ❖ Fiber: 1g

Conclude your dining experience with Mushroom Cream Soup. This dish effortlessly marries the rustic charm of mushrooms with the refinement of cream. Whether enjoying a quiet evening at home or entertaining guests, this recipe from our Slow Cooker Cookbook delivers a profoundly flavorful and creamy soup, ensuring a memorable and luxurious culinary treat.

Recipe 04: Carrot and Pumpkin Cream Soup

Savor the essence of autumn with "Carrot and Pumpkin Cream Soup with Parsley," a warm, inviting dish from our Slow Cooker Cookbook. This soup blends the sweet richness of pumpkin with the earthy tones of carrots; all brought together in a creamy, velvety broth. Perfect for those seeking comfort in a bowl, it offers a nourishing and flavorful escape, promising a soothing and delightful culinary experience with the added freshness of parsley.

Servings: 1

Cook Time: 6 hours

Prepping Time: 15 minutes

Difficulty: Easy

Ingredients:

- ✓ 1 cup pumpkin, cubed
- ✓ 1 cup carrots, chopped
- ✓ 1/2 onion, chopped
- ✓ 2 cups vegetable broth
- ✓ 1/2 cup heavy cream
- ✓ Salt and pepper to taste
- ✓ Fresh parsley, chopped, for garnish

Step-by-Step Preparation:

1. Combine pumpkin, carrots, and onion in the slow cooker.
2. Pour vegetable broth over the vegetables.
3. Cook on low for 6 hours until everything is tender.
4. Puree the soup until smooth.
5. Stir in heavy cream and season with salt and pepper.
6. Serve hot, garnished with fresh parsley.

Nutritional Facts: (Per serving)

- ❖ Calories: 300
- ❖ Protein: 4g
- ❖ Carbohydrates: 25g
- ❖ Fat: 22g
- ❖ Sodium: 500mg
- ❖ Fiber: 6g

Conclude your meal with Carrot and Pumpkin Cream Soup with Parsley, a dish that captures the heartwarming flavors of the season. Whether you need a comforting lunch or a cozy dinner, this recipe from our Slow Cooker Cookbook delivers a beautifully simple yet profoundly satisfying soup, ensuring a memorable and enjoyable dining experience.

Recipe 05: Potato Leek Soup

Embrace the classic comfort of "Potato Leek Soup Garnished with Green Onion," a timeless dish from our Slow Cooker Cookbook. This soup offers a creamy, soothing blend of tender potatoes and mild, sweet leeks, topped with the crisp freshness of green onions. Ideal for those seeking a heartwarming and straightforward meal, it delivers a smooth and flavorful comfort in every spoonful, promising a satisfying and homely culinary experience that's perfect for any occasion.

Servings: 1

Prepping Time: 15 minutes

Cook Time: 6 hours

Difficulty: Easy

Ingredients:

- ✓ 1 cup potatoes, cubed
- ✓ 1 cup leeks, sliced
- ✓ 2 cups vegetable broth
- ✓ 1/2 cup heavy cream
- ✓ Salt and pepper to taste
- ✓ Green onions, chopped, for garnish

Step-by-Step Preparation:

1. Place potatoes and leeks in the slow cooker.
2. Pour vegetable broth over them, ensuring they are fully submerged.
3. Cook on low for 6 hours until potatoes are soft.
4. Blend the mixture until smooth.
5. Stir in heavy cream and adjust seasoning with salt and pepper.
6. Serve hot, garnished with chopped green onions.

Nutritional Facts: (Per serving)

- ❖ Calories: 350
- ❖ Protein: 5g
- ❖ Carbohydrates: 40g
- ❖ Fat: 20g
- ❖ Sodium: 500mg
- ❖ Fiber: 5g

Conclude your dining experience with Potato Leek Soup Garnished with Green Onion. This dish combines comfort food's essence with the simplicity of simple ingredients. Whether you're looking for a cozy lunch or a light dinner, this recipe from our Slow Cooker Cookbook offers a deliciously creamy and satisfying soup, ensuring a delightful and comforting meal.

Recipe 06: Pasta Kielbasa Sausage Soup

Dive into the hearty and robust flavors of "Pasta Kielbasa Sausage Soup," a standout dish from our Slow Cooker Cookbook. This soup combines the savory spice of kielbasa sausage with tender pasta, swimming in a rich broth teeming with vegetables. Perfect for those craving a filling and flavorful meal, it offers a comforting blend of textures and tastes, promising a satisfying and warming dining experience that's as nourishing as it is delicious.

Servings: 1

Prepping Time: 15 minutes

Cook Time: 8 hours

Difficulty: Easy

Ingredients:

- ✓ 1 cup small diced kielbasa sausage
- ✓ 1/2 cup pasta
- ✓ 2 cups beef broth
- ✓ 1/2 cup diced tomatoes
- ✓ 1/4 cup chopped carrots
- ✓ 1/4 cup chopped celery
- ✓ 1/2 onion, chopped
- ✓ 1 garlic clove, minced
- ✓ Salt and pepper to taste
- ✓ Fresh parsley, for garnish

Step-by-Step Preparation:

1. Place kielbasa sausage, carrots, celery, onion, and garlic in the slow cooker.
2. Add diced tomatoes and beef broth.
3. Season with salt and pepper.
4. Cook on low for 8 hours until vegetables are tender.
5. In the last 30 minutes of cooking, add pasta.
6. Serve hot, garnished with fresh parsley.

Nutritional Facts: (Per serving)

- ❖ Calories: 450
- ❖ Protein: 20g
- ❖ Carbohydrates: 40g
- ❖ Fat: 22g
- ❖ Sodium: 950mg
- ❖ Fiber: 3g

Conclude your meal with Pasta Kielbasa Sausage Soup, a dish that encapsulates the essence of hearty cooking. Whether you're looking to warm up on a chilly day or simply in the mood for a comforting bowl of soup, this recipe from our Slow Cooker Cookbook delivers a fulfilling and flavorful experience, ensuring a memorable and cozy culinary delight.

Recipe 07: Laksa Shrimp Soup

Embark on a flavor-packed journey with "Laksa Shrimp Soup - Prawn Noodle Laksa Soup," a vibrant and spicy dish from our Slow Cooker Cookbook. This Southeast Asian delight melds the succulence of shrimp with the aromatic complexity of laksa paste, coconut milk, and a medley of spices, served over tender noodles. It promises a rich tapestry of flavors and textures, perfect for those craving an exotic and satisfying meal. It offers an authentic taste of the region's culinary diversity in every spoonful.

Servings: 1

Cook Time: 4 hours

Prepping Time: 20 minutes

Difficulty: Medium

Ingredients:

- ✓ 1 cup shrimp, peeled
- ✓ 1/2 cup rice noodles
- ✓ 2 cups coconut milk
- ✓ 2 tablespoons laksa paste
- ✓ 1/2 cup bean sprouts
- ✓ 1/4 cup sliced red bell pepper
- ✓ 1 tablespoon fish sauce
- ✓ 1 teaspoon sugar
- ✓ Lime wedges for serving
- ✓ Fresh cilantro for garnish

Step-by-Step Preparation:

1. Mix coconut milk and laksa paste in the slow cooker.
2. Add shrimp, bell pepper, fish sauce, and sugar.
3. Cook on low for 4 hours until flavors meld.
4. Cook rice noodles as per package instructions and add to the soup.
5. Serve hot with bean sprouts, lime wedges, and fresh cilantro.

Nutritional Facts: (Per serving)

- ❖ Calories: 600
- ❖ Protein: 25g
- ❖ Carbohydrates: 50g
- ❖ Fat: 35g
- ❖ Sodium: 1200mg
- ❖ Fiber: 2g

Conclude your dining experience with Laksa Shrimp Soup - Prawn Noodle Laksa Soup, a dish that brings the essence of Southeast Asian cuisine to your table. Whether you're a fan of the region's flavors or exploring new culinary territories, this recipe from our Slow Cooker Cookbook delivers an unforgettable and delectable feast, ensuring a rich and aromatic dining adventure.

Recipe 08: French Onion Soup

Immerse yourself in the comforting depths of "French Onion Soup," a classic dish from our Slow Cooker Cookbook that brings the rich flavors of caramelized onions to the forefront. This recipe expertly combines the sweetness of slow-cooked onions with a savory broth, topped with a golden, melted cheese crust over crusty bread. Ideal for those seeking warmth and comfort in a bowl, it offers a timeless taste experience that soothes the soul and tantalizes the taste buds, promising a cozy and luxurious culinary escape.

Servings: 1

Prepping Time: 15 minutes

Cook Time: 8 hours

Difficulty: Easy

Ingredients:

- ✓ 2 large onions, thinly sliced
- ✓ 4 cups beef broth
- ✓ 1/2 teaspoon thyme
- ✓ 1 bay leaf
- ✓ Salt and pepper to taste
- ✓ 1 slice of crusty bread
- ✓ 1/4 cup grated Gruyère cheese

Step-by-Step Preparation:

1. Place sliced onions in the slow cooker.
2. Add beef broth, thyme, bay leaf, salt, and pepper.
3. Cook on low for 8 hours until onions are caramelized.
4. Toast the bread slice, then place it in a bowl on top of the soup.
5. Sprinkle Gruyère cheese over the bread.
6. Broil until cheese is melted and bubbly.

Nutritional Facts: (Per serving)

- ❖ Calories: 300
- ❖ Protein: 15g
- ❖ Carbohydrates: 35g
- ❖ Fat: 12g
- ❖ Sodium: 900mg
- ❖ Fiber: 4g

Conclude your meal with French Onion Soup, a dish that epitomizes the art of comfort food. Whether enjoyed on a chilly evening or as a starter to a refined dinner, this recipe from our Slow Cooker Cookbook delivers a rich, flavorful, and immensely satisfying experience, ensuring a memorable and comforting dining pleasure.

Recipe 09: Chicken Tortilla Soup

Delve into the bold and vibrant flavors of "Chicken Tortilla Soup Garnished with Shredded Cheddar and Green Onions," a spirited dish from our Slow Cooker Cookbook. This recipe infuses the succulent taste of chicken with a rich blend of tomatoes, spices, and tortillas simmered to perfection. Topped with the sharpness of cheddar and the fresh bite of green onions, it promises a textural and flavorful delight that's as comforting as it is satisfying, offering a hearty and nourishing meal full of character and warmth.

Servings: 1

Prepping Time: 15 minutes

Cook Time: 6 hours

Difficulty: Easy

Ingredients:

- ✓ 1 chicken breast thinly sliced
- ✓ 2 cups chicken broth
- ✓ 1 cup canned diced tomatoes
- ✓ 1/2 onion, chopped
- ✓ 1 garlic clove, minced
- ✓ 1 teaspoon cumin
- ✓ 1/2 teaspoon chili powder
- ✓ Salt and pepper to taste
- ✓ Tortilla strips
- ✓ Shredded cheddar cheese for garnish
- ✓ Green onions, chopped, for garnish

Step-by-Step Preparation:

1. Place chicken, broth, tomatoes, onion, and garlic in the slow cooker.
2. Season with cumin, chili powder, salt, and pepper.
3. Cook on low for 6 hours until chicken is tender.
4. Shred the chicken and return it to the soup.
5. Serve hot, topped with tortilla strips, shredded cheddar, and green onions.

Nutritional Facts: (Per serving)

- ❖ Calories: 400
- ❖ Protein: 35g
- ❖ Carbohydrates: 25g
- ❖ Fat: 18g
- ❖ Sodium: 800mg
- ❖ Fiber: 3g

Conclude your dining experience with Chicken Tortilla Soup, a dish that brings a taste of the Southwest to your table. Whether you're seeking a comforting lunch or a casual dinner, this recipe from our Slow Cooker Cookbook delivers a deliciously layered and profoundly satisfying soup, ensuring a flavorful and heartwarming culinary journey.

Recipe 10: Thick Milky Clam Chowder Soup

Savor the luxurious embrace of "Thick Milky Clam Chowder Soup," a masterpiece from our Slow Cooker Cookbook that combines the best of the sea's offerings. This rich and hearty soup marries succulent clams and prawns with a creamy, velvety base, creating a symphony of flavors and textures. Perfect for seafood lovers seeking comfort in a bowl, it delivers a satisfyingly thick chowder that warms the heart and delights the palate, promising an indulgent dining experience that's both sophisticated and comforting.

Servings: 1

Prepping Time: 20 minutes

Cook Time: 4 hours

Difficulty: Easy

Ingredients:

- ✓ 1/2 cup canned clams, drained
- ✓ 1/2 cup prawns, peeled and deveined
- ✓ 1 cup diced potatoes
- ✓ 1/2 cup diced celery
- ✓ 1/2 cup diced carrots
- ✓ 2 cups milk
- ✓ 1 cup heavy cream
- ✓ 1/2 onion, finely chopped
- ✓ 1 tablespoon flour
- ✓ Salt and pepper to taste
- ✓ Fresh parsley for garnish

Step-by-Step Preparation:

1. Layer potatoes, celery, carrots, and onion in the slow cooker.
2. Mix flour with some milk to create a smooth paste, then combine with the rest of the milk and pour over the vegetables.
3. Add clams and prawns, season with salt and pepper.
4. Cook on low for 4 hours until everything is tender.
5. Stir in heavy cream in the last half-hour of cooking.
6. Garnish with fresh parsley before serving.

Nutritional Facts: (Per serving)

- ❖ Calories: 750
- ❖ Protein: 30g
- ❖ Carbohydrates: 55g
- ❖ Fat: 45g
- ❖ Sodium: 650mg
- ❖ Fiber: 5g

Conclude your meal with Thick Milky Clam Prawn Chowder Soup, a dish that brings the essence of the ocean right to your table. Whether enjoyed as a sumptuous starter or a main course, this recipe from our Slow Cooker Cookbook offers a decadent, creamy delight that will satisfy any craving for seafood chowder, ensuring a memorable and cozy culinary experience.

CONCLUSION

As you turn the final page of "Delicious Slow Cooker Recipes for One: Quick and Healthy Meals Cookbook with Mouthwatering Pictures," reflect on the journey you've embarked upon with Clara Levine. This cookbook has equipped you with an array of recipes tailored for solo dining and transformed your approach to cooking and eating.

Each recipe has been carefully curated to ensure that cooking for one is a joy, not a chore. From the simplicity of preparation to the diversity of flavors, this book has shown that healthy eating can be accessible and enjoyable. The stunning pictures have served as a visual guide and inspiration to explore and experiment with new dishes.

Now, equipped with various recipes, from comforting soups to decadent desserts, you have the tools to make every meal an opportunity to treat yourself. The ease and convenience of slow cooking mean you can enjoy wholesome, delicious meals without the fuss, making it easier to stick to healthy eating habits.

Let "Delicious Slow Cooker Recipes for One" continue as your culinary companion. Revisit your favorite recipes and challenge yourself to try new ones. Share your culinary creations and the joy of slow cooking with friends and family. If this book has enhanced your dining experience, consider exploring more of Clara Levine's culinary collections. Remember, every meal is a chance to nourish not just your body but also your soul. Keep cooking, experimenting, and, most importantly, enjoying every bite!

Made in United States
Troutdale, OR
09/27/2024

23162808R00060